95/8/-

D0925817

Indian Women and the Law in Canada:

Citizens Minus

by
Kathleen Jamieson

April 1978

the National Film Board.

This document expresses the views
of the author and does not
necessarily represent the official
policy of the ACSW.

© Minister of Supply and Services Canada 1978

Catalogue No. LW31-2/1978
ISBN 0-662-01854-0

Preface

When native women in Canada realized that there was no documentation of the discrimination against us we requested the assistance of the Advisory Council on the Status of Women. We asked them to work with us jointly in our efforts to prepare this documentation.

Social and psychological losses faced by our enfranchised women can never be fully assessed, but the joint efforts in this study are a major step in this direction.

We thank the author for her extensive research in this issue that has plagued our native women for the last 109 years. Our deepest gratitude to the Advisory Council on the Status of Women, in the completion of this study.

We trust the Great Spirit to help Indian leaders and legislators expedite the removal of discriminatory practices such as Section 12(1)(b) in the Indian Act.

Jenny Margetts
IRIW

Contents

Chapter 1

The Status of Indian Women —
Moral Dilemma or Political Expediency?

For one hundred and nine years Indian women in Canada have been subject to a law which discriminates against them on the grounds of race, sex and marital status. The Indian Act, which regulates the position of Indians in Canada, provides that an Indian woman who marries a non-Indian man ceases to be an Indian within the meaning of any statute or law in Canada.[1]

The consequences for the Indian woman of the application of section 12(1)(b) of the Indian Act extend from marriage to the grave — and even beyond that. The woman, on marriage, must leave her parents' home and her reserve. She may not own property on the reserve and must dispose of any property she does hold. She may be prevented from inheriting property left to her by her parents. She cannot take any further part in band business. Her children are not recognized as Indian and are therefore denied access to cultural and social amenities of the Indian community. And, most punitive of all, she may be prevented from returning to live with her family on the reserve, even if she is in dire need, very ill, a widow, divorced or separated. Finally, her body may not be buried on the reserve with those of her forebears.[2]

The deleterious effects of this oppressive legislation on the Indian woman and her children materially, culturally and psychologically can be very grave indeed.

No such restrictions are provided in the Indian Act for Indian men, who may marry whom they please without penalty and indeed by so doing confer on their non-Indian spouses and children full Indian rights and status.

Other Canadian women do not face such severe penalties on marriage. They may return if and when they wish to their parents' home, they are not subject to restrictions on inheritance of property, and even if married to a citizen of a foreign country they are able to confer Canadian citizenship on their children.[3]

The Indian Act is now being revised through a process of consultation between the government and the National Indian Brotherhood, but Indian women who have lost their status have been denied a voice in these negotiations. This study, undertaken at the request of the National Committee of Indian Rights for Indian Women, is intended to document the legislation which deprives women of their Indian status, to analyze the development of this policy, and to determine the consequences for Indian women and their children. In this way it is hoped to support their efforts to regain the full equality of status with Indian men to which their Indian birth entitles them.

The particular focus of this study is derived from an examination of the present impasse between government and Indian leaders on this issue. Both sides admit that the discrimination against Indian women is manifestly unjust, but neither the government nor the Indian leaders have yet been able to agree on how this question might be resolved.

The consultative process, by way of a joint committee of the Cabinet and the National Indian Brotherhood (NIB) has been going on since 1975. But until December 1977, when the topic of band membership was briefly broached, Indian women's loss of status had not even been mentioned and had been regarded, as if by tacit and mutual consent of all concerned, as too "delicate" to discuss.[4]

Such attitudes undoubtedly had their origin in the Lavell case, which established for both sides the inviolateness of the Indian Act. The case, which became a political vehicle for both the government and the Indians, came before the Supreme Court of Canada in 1973, when Jeannette Lavell contested her loss of Indian Status under section 12(1)(b) of the Indian Act. The basis of the case (which is discussed in detail in Chapter 14) was that the discriminatory provisions of this section of the Indian Act were contrary to the Canadian Bill of Rights.

The government had just published a "White Paper" proposing that the Indian Act should be phased out.[5] But a strong Indian political front was emerging, apparently determined to wring from the government redress for past injustices. Insistence on the retention of the Indian Act was regarded as a crucial part of this strategy by the Indian leaders. As Harold Cardinal put it, "We do not want the Indian Act retained because it is a good piece of legislation, it isn't. It is discriminatory from start to finish. But it is a lever in our hands and an embarrassment to the government, as it should be. . . . We would rather continue to live in bondage under the *Indian Act* than surrender our sacred rights."[6] The Indian Act was thus transformed from the legal instrument of oppression which it had been since its inception into a repository of sacred rights for Indians. The opposition of Indian leaders to the claim of Lavell became a matter of policy to be pursued at all cost by government and Indians together because it endangered the Indian Act.

Jeannette Lavell lost her case, but the consequences were far-reaching. The issue of Indian women's status under section 12(1)(b) acquired, for many people, the dimensions of a moral dilemma — the rights of all Indians against the rights of a minority of Indians, i.e. Indian women. The case created a united Indian front on the "untouchable" nature of the Indian Act. And finally, the federal government's

2

eagerness to support the major Indian political associations (most of which seem to have almost exclusively male executives and memberships) against Lavell established a basis for continued government-Indian interaction, which had been in deadlock since the conflict over the government "White Paper" of 1969. The rapport generated during the Lavell case was, after a short period of gestation, to give birth in 1975 to a joint NIB-Cabinet consultative committee to revise the Indian Act.

The government gave an undertaking to the NIB that no part of the Indian Act would be changed until revision of the whole Act is complete, after full process of consultation. The result of this gentlemen's agreement has been that until very recently, a powerful blanket of silence was imposed on discussion of the status of Indian women and the topic began to assume an extra dimension. It became taboo and unwise in certain circles even to mention the subject. Despite the fact that the Indian Act continues to discriminate against them on the basis of race, sex and marital status, and is contrary to the most fundamental principles of human rights, Indian women who have dared to speak out against it have been seen by many as somehow threatening the "human rights" of Indians as a whole.

The fact that Indian women in Canada who have lost their status are expected to accept this oppression compounds and perpetuates the injustice and has clear parallels in other societies where discriminatory practices and legislation permit the victimization of one group by another.

"The concept of 'Victimization'," according to St. Clair Drake, "implies that some people are used as a means to other people's ends — without their consent — and that the social system is so structured that it can be deliberately manipulated to the disadvantage of some groups by the clever, the vicious and the cynical as well as by the powerful. The callous and the indifferent unconsciously and unintentionally reinforce the system by their inaction or inertia. The 'victims', their autonomy curtailed and their self-esteem weakened by the operation of the caste-class system, are confronted with identity problems; their social condition is essentially one of powerlessness."[7] It is also typical that in such a system any attempt by the victim to alleviate oppression is seen as an attempt to subvert the system.

The concept of "victimization" articulated above, although developed in U.S. contexts, has clear application to the historical position of Indians in Canadian society and most certainly to the position of Indian women in Canada today. Indian women have not only been historically "victimized" but they are subject to psychological pressure from both government and Indian leaders to keep silent and to accept their position as "martyrs for a cause", in fact apotheosizing their own oppression until the whole Indian Act is revised.

Each side claims that it is faced with a moral dilemma. The government insists that it would like to change the law, but that this would be contrary to the wishes of the Indian people. It has therefore

3

deliberately excluded the Indian Act from the provisions of the new Human Rights Act, which came into force on March 1st, 1978, thus preventing any possibility of appeal against discrimination in the Indian Act by Indian women.[8]

The Indian leaders, on the other hand, claim that their mistrust of government's intentions is so great that they cannot agree to any section of the Indian Act being changed or even temporarily suspended until the whole Act is completely revised.[9]

A curious twist to the issue has now developed. Despite the fact that section 12(1)(b) is part of an Indian Act which was developed by previous federal governments without consultation with the Indian people, and despite the fact that this kind of discrimination against Indian women was never part of Indian cultural tradition, as later chapters of this study will show, the government is now placing the onus for the continuing existence of this discrimination squarely on the shoulders of the Indians and their representatives, the NIB.

Thus we find in a nationally-read newspaper the recent headline: "Indians' leaders warned to halt discrimination against women." The article then begins, "Justice Minister Ronald Basford has warned Indian leaders that Parliament is not going to tolerate 'for too long' the discrimination against women contained in the Indian Act."[10]

The Honourable Marc Lalonde, the Minister responsible for the Status of Women, in February 1978, informed a meeting of women delegates from across Canada that the issue of discrimination against Indian women is complicated and that "Discrimination against women is a scandal but imposing the cultural standards of white society on native society would be another scandal."[11]

This "two scandals" argument is another version of the "moral dilemma", but this time discrimination against women is argued as being Indian custom and for the government to impose other values prohibiting discrimination would be scandalous.

Of the many and varied arguments that have been used to justify the continued existence of this legislation, this product of the 1970s is the most insidious.

For the Indians themselves this is now a very divisive issue. To arrive at any consensus of opinion in the near future which will be acceptable to Indians across Canada seems an almost hopeless task. Yet the longer this law remains, the more divisive and the more difficult to resolve it becomes.

Recent statements by Noel Starblanket, President of the National Indian Brotherhood, indicate a change of heart on his part, though not necessarily of the NIB. Starblanket has stated quite unequivocally that the Indian Act unfairly discriminates against women and that he does not want to see the issue buried but researched and clarified so that an equitable solution might be found.[12]

4

Dimensions of the Problem

In order to explain adequately the evolution of the legislation for Indian women this study takes a historical and sociological approach to the problem.

The emphasis is on the complex and changing attitudes to Indian women. The laws controlling intermarriage between Indian women and white men are put in a context of broader historical trends. By so doing it is hoped to arrive at a better understanding of the perceptions and prejudices that generated different laws for Indians and whites and Indian men and Indian women in the past, as well as their retention today.

Implicit in the analysis in this study is a more general conceptual framework in which the 1869 legislation, which first introduced a section penalizing Indian women who married non-Indians, is seen as having arisen not as a function of the reserve system and necessity to protect reserve land, but as part of the government policy of assimilation. And this is seen here as part of what may be described as a developing caste/class system in which society became more and more stratified and inequality on the basis of race and social class had become an organizing principle. The extra dimension of institutionalized sexual inequality ensured for Indian women in the mid-nineteenth century a very special place right at the bottom of this hierarchical structure.

Restrictions on marriages between races are a manifestation of a complex blend of notions based on race, class and sexual inequality. There are variations on the theme but the basic elements remain the same today as in 1869. This is most clearly demonstrated in the United States, where in many states inter-racial marriages were illegal until 1967. Even when the climate of public opinion seemed in favour of racial equality inter-racial marriage was still viewed negatively.[13]

Though (unlike the U.S. then and South Africa today) Canadian legislation has provided sanctions only for the Indian woman in the event of inter-racial marriage, the expressed views of the majority of the Canadian Supreme Court in the Lavell case indicate a similarly cautious, conservative approach to this whole question of race and sex and the deep prejudice these topics trigger in the Canadian public. It is the resultant "inaction or inertia" on the part of the Canadian public which permits the continued "victimization" of Indian women described earlier.

Each dimension of this problem — race, class and sexual inequality — is as powerful and deeply entrenched a force in Canadian society today as in the nineteenth century. The historical approach is thus implicitly intended to show also how these dimensions varied with each other over time to create specific government policies and legislation at given periods.

This approach indicates a threefold focus of inquiry:

1) Government legislation, policy and attitudes towards intermarriage between white men and Indian women,
2) Government legislation and policy for all Indians,
3) Indian tradition and Indian reaction to government policy and administration.

All of these are very broad topics and single aspects of each of them have been the subject of lengthy treatises. Nevertheless it does not seem possible to view any of these three elements in isolation and to arrive at a meaningful interpretation of the evolution of the legislation of 1869 or its subsequent elaborations. The broad approach, however, makes it possible to demonstrate that attitudes towards intermarriage and Indian women and the restrictive laws were indeed part of a much broader development in ethnic, sex and class relations in nineteenth century Canada, and it provides a basis for unravelling and refuting the arguments for the continuing oppression of Indian women today.

Chapter 2

The Indian Act View of Women

Section 11 of the amended 1951 Indian Act, which is the Act in force today, defines who is an Indian for the purposes of the Act in the following terms:

"11. (1) Subject to section 12, a person is entitled to be registered if that person

(a) on the 26th day of May 1874 was, for the purposes of An Act providing for the organization of the Department of the Secretary of State of Canada, and for the management of Indian and Ordnance Lands, being chapter 42 of the Statutes of Canada, 1868, as amended by section 6 of chapter 6 of the Statutes of Canada, 1869, and section 8 of chapter 21 of the Statutes of Canada, 1874, considered to be entitled to hold, use or enjoy the lands and other immovable property belonging to or appropriated to the use of the various tribes, bands or bodies of Indians in Canada;

(b) is a member of a band

   (i) for whose use and benefit, in common, lands have been set apart or since the 26th of May 1874, have been agreed by treaty to be set apart, or

   (ii) that has been declared by the Governor in Council to be a band for the purposes of this Act;

(c) is a *male** person who is a direct descendant in the *male* line of a *male* person described in paragraph (a) or (b);

(d) is the legitimate child of

   (i) *a male* person described in paragraph (a) or (b), or

   (ii) a person described in paragraph (c);

(e) is the illegitimate child of a female person described in paragraph (a), (b) or (d); or

(f) is the wife or widow of a person who is entitled to be registered by virtue of paragraph (a), (b), (c), (d) or (e)."[1]

When the male bias in this section is then read in conjunction with section 12, which defines who is not entitled to be registered as an Indian, it becomes evident that the Act is designed to discriminate between Indian men and Indian women and that Indian women are not entitled to enjoy the same Indian rights as Indian men.

*Emphasis added.

7

This is most clearly set out in section 12(1)(b) of the Act which states:

"12.(1) The following persons are not entitled to be registered, namely...
(b) a woman who married a person who is not an Indian, unless that
woman is subsequently the wife or widow of a person described in
section 11."[2]

The "person who is not an Indian" means any man who is not considered to have Indian status for the purposes of the Indian Act. The woman who marries such a person is automatically deprived of her Indian status and her band rights from the date of her marriage. In addition, an Indian woman who marries a member of another band is transferred to the band of her husband regardless of her wishes. If she moves from a prosperous band to a poor band, she may find herself deprived of monies in the form of revenues which she feels are her birthright. She also loses other rights which adhere to membership of the band into which she was born. Even if a woman does not marry, any child she may have may be deprived of Indian status if upon protest to the Registrar it is determined that the father of the child was not an Indian.[3]

Early legislation for Indians did not make such invidious distinctions between male and female Indians. The earliest Indian Acts dating from the middle of the nineteenth century were enacted to deal with Indians on reserves.[4] These reserves were created usually, though not always, as the result of treaties made with the Indians in which they ceded their lands for settlement to the British government (the Crown) in return for a portion of land — the reserve — and certain other benefits. It eventually became necessary to enact legislation detailing who was entitled to these benefits and to live on the reserves. But it was not until after Confederation, in the Indian Act of 1869, that the forerunners of the present sections 11 and 12(1)(b) setting out a separate legal regime for Indian women were incorporated in the legislation.[5] Since then, the provisions of the Indian Act relating to Indian women have become increasingly restrictive in content and more punitive in tone.

The 1869 legislation was created primarily on the basis of the Dominion Government experience with the Iroquois and Algonquin groups of Ontario and Quebec. It was only *after* the framework and much of the substance of the Indian Act were in place that it was extended uniformly across Canada in the Act of 1874 and in later Acts to include all Indians as the various provinces came into Confederation.[6] The great diversity of lifestyles and forms of social organization of the Indians west of Ontario were not considered an important factor in law-making in 1869.

The key question then remains: to what extent did the provisions of the law which related to women accord with the customary position of married women among Iroquois and Algonquian Indians for whom the law was made?

Iroquois traditional culture seems to have been fairly homogeneous and fortunately has been well documented in the contemporary accounts of travellers and missionaries as well as by many ethnographers who have drawn on Indian as well as European sources.

To what extent this tradition could indeed be said to be that which was still strong in 1869 is more complex. Certainly the Iroquois at the Caughnawaga Reserve in Quebec, which had been set up and controlled by Jesuit missionaries in the mid-seventeenth century and since then had attracted refugees and Christian converts from many different Indian groups,[7] could be expected to have evolved a rather different kind of society from the Iroquois of the Six Nations in southern Ontario, who had their own complex and chequered history of migrations in the eighteenth century and of prolonged contact with both Protestant missionaries and the military.[8]

Nevertheless many authorities seem to agree that for many centuries before the nineteenth century and possibly for a part of that century also Iroquois society was matrifocal, descent was traced matrilineally (i.e. through women) and post-marital residence was matrilocal (i.e., after marriage the husband went to live with his wife's family). Each dwelling, traditionally a longhouse,[9] was owned by a senior woman, and in it lived her spouse, their daughters and spouses and their children. If a woman did not want her husband to continue living in her house she simply "tossed his personal effects out of the door of the longhouse" and so divorced him. The children remained with the mother. Subsistence was obtained from the practice of horticulture. Corn, beans and squash were the main crops, with the women organizing, jointly owning and working the gardens and also distributing the produce. Fishing rights also were held by the women. The men hunted, engaged in constant warfare (in historical times at least) and were usually away for long periods of time.[10]

In the political sphere the senior matrons elected and deposed the elders of the Council, the highest ruling body of the league of the Iroquois (traditionally founded in 1570). Hereditary eligibility to this Council was through the female. Goldenweiser in 1912 described the role of the women in the selection of a new chief when a chief had died thus:

> "When a chief died, the women of his tribe and clan held a meeting at which a candidate for the vacant place was decided upon. A woman delegate carried the news to the chiefs of the clans which belonged to the 'side' of the deceased chief's clan. They had the power to veto the selection, in which case another women's meeting was called and another candidate selected . . . "[11]

According to Schoolcraft the matrons also had veto powers in questions of war and peace.[12]

In 1724, Lafitau, basing his statements on personal experience and the "Jesuit Relations", made this unequivocal comment on the position of women: "Nothing, however, is more real than this superiority of the women. It is of them that the nation really consists; and it is through them that the nobility of the blood, the genealogical tree and the families

9

are perpetuated. All real authority is vested in them. The land, the fields and their harvest all belong to them . . . the children are their domain and it is through their blood that the order of succession is transmitted."[13]

Much of the literature relating to Iroquois women has been summarized by Judith Brown in a paper entitled "Iroquois Women: An Ethnohistoric Note". Brown's thesis is that Iroquois women's economic contribution and their control of the distribution of all food, even that procured by men, was the key to their powerful role in politics and religion.[14]

European social organization was clearly quite different from this in many fundamental respects. Though women did in fact contribute substantially to subsistence through paid labour they had little or no personal or political autonomy.[15] For most of the nineteenth century a married woman's wages and property belonged to her husband. The unmarried minor female came under the aegis of her father or male guardian. The older unmarried females — spinsters and widows — were despised social anomalies. But if propertied they had some civil though not political rights.[16]

But what of the other major Indian group to whom the 1869 legislation applied — the Algonquians? Unlike the Iroquois they are not a homogeneous group and so it is not possible to generalize much. Theye were usually, however, hunting and gathering people, nomadic and nucleated into small independent groups with, usually, little formal political or social organization. Post-marital residence patterns and descent reckoning were very varied, it is now generally agreed. But it should be noted that until a decade ago anthropologists writing on hunters and gatherers such as the Algonquians have assumed that patrilineal descent and patrilocal residence were the most prevalent type of small community or band organization among virtually all North American hunters and gatherers prior to contact.[17]

Influential theorists who have developed typologies based on this assumption, such as Julian Steward, one of the fathers of American anthropology, and his pupil Elman Service, had grounded their theories on supposed bioeconomic premises — 1) that male dominance is innate, and 2) the greater economic importance of the male in a hunting and gathering society.[18] This was substantiated by data from the early theoretical writings on Australian Aborigines of the "father of British social anthropology", Radcliffe-Brown,[19] who worked from similar assumptions. Recent research however has shown that in most pedestrian hunting and gathering economies, including that of the Australian Aborigines and those found in Canada, gathering contributes more to subsistence than hunting.[20] In fact, in most hunting and gathering societies women contribute between 60% and 80% of subsistence.[21] Only in arctic and sub-arctic areas were the textbook examples of mammal hunters found and early typologies of forms of social organization were not based on studies of these groups.

However, even where hunting is the primary subsistence base, an anthropologist, Eleanor Leacock, writing on the Montagnais Naskapi on the basis of her own field work and information in the "Jesuit Relations" has found a strong case for matrilocal residence.[22]

Bioeconomics are thus seen to be a very shaky basis for inferring social organization.

More recently researchers have agreed that there can be no consensus on which kind of kinship or post-marital residence pattern prevailed among Algonquian hunters and gatherers pre-contact. The impact of the fur trade and European settlement on nomadic groups remains incalculable. Ethnographic consideration of social organization is therefore limited by the fact that, whatever the findings, they are most likely nothing more than, according to anthropologist Kay Markin, "a pot-pourri of adaptations to rapidly changing ecological circumstances"[23] — territorial displacement and severe reduction in the availability of animal and vegetable resources.

Only in the 1970s, however, have social scientists begun to realize what profound implications such findings on patterns of social organization and the role of woman in subsistence have for the study of human relations. Paul Samuelson of the Massachusetts Institute of Technology has summarized very neatly the importance of this for economic analysis, for example, as well as their general acceptance in an introductory economics text.

> "From the dawn of recorded history, we find that women have played an important role in producing the G.N.P. Among human societies, as among animal species, there have been many alternative patterns of specialization with respect to foraging, herding, planting and sowing. Only in the art of warfare have men shown any unique talent — and that claim could be disputed. Indeed in many societies that anthropologists have studied, it has been women who have produced virtually all of the G.N.P., men filling at best the role of an attractive nuisance. Particularly in self sufficient agriculture, whether of Old World peasantry or New World frontier, it has been quite impossible to differentiate between the cooperative roles of men and women in producing the G.N.P. Patterns of dominance, as between patriarchal and matriarchal systems, have shown no close relation to economic organization and performance."[24]

This final sentence should be qualified, perhaps, since some recent studies have, as Judith Brown suggested in her paper, shown a correlation between the so-called 'matriarchal' systems and economic organization.[25]

In mid-Victorian Canada such notions concerning the role of women would have been given short shrift by most legislators. (These men were not likely to be impressed by Bachofen, Morgan or Engels, then writing on matriarchal societies.)[26] They had no doubts at all about "the natural order of things" and their beliefs were firmly grounded in a patriarchal system in which the ideal woman, "the lady", was a delicate, swooning ornament totally dependent on and subservient to the male, who alone was capable of working outside the home. This, of course, made the vast majority of women, the working poor in factories, in the fields, in mines and in domestic service, something less than the ideal woman, and also devalued the worth of their contribution in their own eyes as well as in the eyes of the rest of society.[27]

Thus reports in 1845 and 1880 that Indian women did much of the work and provided for their families in Upper and Lower Canada were met with surprise and generated criticism of the Indian male, who declined to take over what he saw as the woman's role but because of the effect of European settlement was unable to carry on his traditional role of hunting or warring.[28]

Those who formulated legislation for Indians in the nineteenth century were not, it would seem, given to much soul-searching about what was the custom. Indeed this was not even relevant since they were quite convinced of the natural superiority of European culture and the decadence of most Indian traditions.

European cultural values, which served as a model for the development of the early laws relating to Indians, were based primarily on the needs of an agricultural society. The notions of private rights in land inherited through the male were an indispensible component of this system, which had as its corollary control and repression of the sexuality of the female. Only thus could it be assumed that property was inherited by the correct heir. The threat that women's autonomy posed to this system resulted in the development of a body of common law emphasizing the importance of legitimacy and the legal ownership by a husband of a wife's generative capacity. The wife was in common law the property of her husband. Work (labour for pay) and the accumulation of goods were seen as an end in themselves.[29] Christianity was held to endorse and reinforce these principles in Scripture. The Indian married woman was thus seen as an appendage to her husband whether he was Indian or white.

But these European cultural precepts of the importance of private property and inheritance through the male, along with repression of female sexuality and "work" as an end in itself — and incidentally as a male prerogative — were not customary for the Indians of Eastern Canada, for whom this legislation was devised, nor did it represent the wishes of the Indians concerned.

Indians have never been a party to formulating any section of the Indian Act. They were not consulted in 1869 nor have they ever, until now, been concerned in the drafting of legislation for Indians. As to the particular section penalizing women who "marry out", historical documents cited later in this paper show that from the beginning, Indians in the East, and then in the West as the treaties were being made, were strongly opposed to legal discrimination against Indian women and their children, who married non-Indians.

The 1869 legislation which introduced this discrimination was intended as a measure to reduce the number of Indians and halfbreeds on reserves as part of the government's stated policy of doing away with reserves and of assimilating all native people into the Euro-Canadian culture. Indeed, the whole of nineteenth century legislation for Indians was based on the assumption that Indians were to be gradually "civilized", to be assimilated by this superior culture, and that in the meantime special laws were required to regulate their transition from barbarism to this state of grace.

Assimilation meant the phasing out of separate Indian status and the gradual absorption of all Indians into the Euro-Canadian population. This was to be accomplished through a process of accustoming Indians to European lifestyles, customs, beliefs and values. The culmination of this process was the act of enfranchising. Enfranchisement meant that an Indian was no longer an Indian in law, had become civilized and was entitled to all the rights and responsibilities of other

Canadian citizens. (It was indeed not possible until 1956 to remain an Indian and be a Canadian citizen.) Euro-Canadian culture was clearly considered by Euro-Canadians in the nineteenth century, at least, infinitely superior to Indian. Indians however did not want to relinquish their own cultures and resisted assimilation as best they could.[30]

Chapter 3

Changing Attitudes to Intermarriage

In order to see how the policy of assimilation was first developed, it is necessary to go back in time to the period of early European contact with the Indians.

The two colonial powers in North America, the French and British, differed in their policies towards Indians in this early time. The French from the very beginning envisaged assimilation of the Indians as the ultimate goal.[1] The British, on the other hand, had no such objectives prior to the nineteenth century.[2] But the policy of assimilation for both the French and later the British was essentially the same and meant christianizing and "civilizing" to European cultural ideals.

Assimilation for the French, however, also included an official policy of intermarrying with the Indians to alleviate the shortage of French women and expand the new French population. Champlain in his "Voyages" of 1613 says he "promised" the Huron Indians that the French would intermarry with them.[3]

The Indians, however, didn't think this was necessarily such a good idea — Cornelius Jaenen quotes an Indian chief, Tadoussac, who replied to charges that his people were not intermarrying because they disliked the French by saying, ". . . What more do you want? I believe that some of these days you'll be asking for our wives. You are continually asking us for our children but you do not give us yours; I do not know any family among us which keeps a Frenchman with it."[4] In other words, Tadoussac didn't care very much for this one-way exchange.

A practice was then adopted of giving dowries to Indian girls to encourage stable marriages with Frenchmen, and this "Présent du Roi" had the blessing of Louis XIV.[5] But despite these efforts the policy wasn't very successful in creating more Frenchmen. Instead, children of these marriages and of more casual encounters with Indian women (which were more frequent) were usually absorbed into the mother's group.[6]

The Jesuits, a strong and influential presence in New France from the early days, had always disapproved of this policy. Their first priority was conversion to Christianity, and they did not associate it with assimilation. The French government was aware of this and Colbert in 1668 is recorded as having warned the Intendant, Bouterone, to beware of the Jesuits' preference for racial segregation.[7] Indeed there seemed to have developed some conflict between the priorities of the State and those of the Church. The two policies nevertheless were two sides of the same coin. When government-promoted intermarriage didn't result in assimilation and Jesuit education of the children failed to gain lasting conversions to Christianity there was unanimous agreement that the Indians' way of life must change and that they should be encouraged to give up their nomadic lifestyle and become sedentary farmers before any real change could be effected. Segregation on reservations, which the Jesuits had already been experimenting with in South America, was then advocated as the most effective device for achieving this end.[8]

Thus was created the first Indian reserve — a laboratory with a missionary-controlled environment in which the desired changes in the Indians could be effected. The reservation at Sillery planned in 1635 by Jean le Jeune became the first of a long line of experiments aimed at changing the ways of the North American Indians. Other reserves soon followed at St. Maurice River near Trois-Rivières, Lorette and Sault St. Louis (Caughnawaga).[9]

The basis of the early economy of New France was the fur trade with the Indians and until 1660 the French had a virtual monopoly, controlling access to the territories in the American North and West. In 1660 this monopoly ended when the Company of Adventurers of Hudson's Bay was founded by the Royal Charter of King Charles II. The British then entered the Hudson's Bay area, built trading posts, and began to compete with the French for the trade with the Indians. After 1714, following on the defeat of the French in Europe and the Treaty of Utrecht, the British had a monopoly of the fur trade in Hudson's Bay.[10]

The policy of the Hudson's Bay Company towards Indians was quite explicitly articulated at the very beginning. Strict segregation was enjoined and neither colonization nor assimilation nor Christianization was of the least interest to the directors of the Company. They had only one motive — to make a profit. Paramilitary trading posts were seen as the most efficient way to achieve this, and men only were recruited in Britain and shipped out to serve for periods of a few years at a time at the posts.[11]

But despite all regulations to the contrary, liaisons between these men and Indian women became very frequent. During the eighteenth century there developed a recognized form of marriage "à la façon du pays" which was adapted from a blend of Indian and European custom and which might last only as long as the trader was in "Indian Country" or for a lifetime if he chose to stay.[12] And more of the men did choose to stay on as the century progressed. The children of these marriages, according to anthropologist Jennifer Brown, were defined

16

as Indian when they were assimilated among the Indians around the post and "English" when they had received an English education.[13]

By the turn of the century such unions were still not officially recognized by the London Committee of the Hudson's Bay Company, and in 1802 a Fort York committee wrote to the London Committee requesting it to reconsider its objection to Indian women at the Fort, emphasizing at some length their economic contribution. It was evident from this letter that intermarriage "à la façon du pays" was already well established.[14]

Indeed Indian women possessed a number of skills which made their economic contribution considerable and presence indispensable around the fort as well as on journeys. Most important were the making of snowshoes and skin clothing, the cleaning and dressing of hides and the preservation of meat — all vital to survival in the Canadian winter and skills unlikely to be part of the repertoire of the average Hudson's Bay servant.[15] Indian women also acted as interpreters, guides and ambassadors to other Indian groups.[16]

To insist on categorizing these relationships as being primarily based on the sexual exploitation of Indian women does not accord with documented facts. This view is clearly based on the old double standard of what was appropriate sexual behaviour for males and females as well as its Victorian corollary which ascribed for women a purely sexual identity and three possible roles in life: virgin, mother or whore.

Extensive evidence concerning these unions is documented in the report of the famous case of Johnstone v. Connolly of 1869.[17] This case established the legal validity of such marriages and indeed was held as a precedent for establishing the validity of all customary marriages until 1951.[18]

Most interesting in this case was that the "customary" marriage of John Connolly to an Indian woman was upheld as valid over a second marriage to a wealthy Montreal woman, Julia Woolrich, which was contracted in 1832 in a church, with all legal formalities carefully observed, but while Suzanne, the Indian wife by a customary marriage of 1803, was still alive. What was crucial in winning this case was the existence of several witnesses, fur traders mainly, who gave testimony, documenting and describing from their own experience that customary marriages were usually monogamous, undertaken freely by both parties and of long duration.[19]

About 1830, however, it was clear that such unions were being rejected by "men of station" such as Governor Simpson and his friend McTavish and the man in the case, John Connolly.[20]

Unfortunately, history has until very recently concerned itself almost exclusively with the lives and opinions of famous men and it is therefore the bleak views of Governor Simpson expressed in his influential writings which have prevailed and have created a stereotype of the

Indian woman as the exploited concubine of the white man or as a pawn of Indian men handed over to cement trading alliances with white men.

Sylvia Van Kirk, writing on fur trade women, quotes a letter written in 1825 in which Simpson demonstrated his disapproval while recognizing that customary marriage was universally accepted in fur trade society. It should be understood "in the outset that nearly all the Gentlemen & Servants have families altho' Marriage ceremonies are unknown in this Country and that it would be all in vain to attempt breaking through this uncivilized custom".[21]

He was very surprised ("appalled" according to Van Kirk) at the degree of control that the Indian and Métis women had over their white husbands. Writing in his journal of 1824-25 he made this clear: "It is not surprising that the Columbia Department is unprofitable ... but ... with the necessary spirit of enterprise and a disregard to little domestic comforts it may be a most productive branch of the Company's trade ... it must be understood that to effect this change we have no petty coat politicians, that is, that Chief Facters (sic) and Chief Traders do not allow themselves to be influenced by the Sapient Councils of their *Squaws* (the emphasis is Simpson's) or neglect their business merely to administer to the comforts and guard against the indiscretions which these frail brown ones are so apt to indulge in."[22] Other epithets applied to Indian women by Simpson were "copper cold-mate", "my article" or "my Japan help-mate" (in reference to an earlier native wife, Betsey).[23] Simpson, it would seem then, not only introduced a strong emphasis on social class but a distinct note of racial prejudice which became increasingly the hallmark of Anglo-colonial relations everywhere as the nineteenth century progressed.[24]

Simpson nevertheless was in fact expressing sentiments that were to become more and more prevalent in eastern Canada as time went on. In the 1830s fur traders with social aspirations and in constant contact with a new wealthy quasi-aristocracy in Montreal society began to feel the pressure to conform. Governor Simpson, however, shocked Red River society when he returned with an upper class English bride to Red River in 1830. He had not bothered to inform either his colleagues or his Indian wife, who had borne him a child while he was away.[25]

A few other leading traders who had close contacts with eastern society soon followed his lead. But for the great majority of the men and women at the posts in the interior life carried on very much as before for quite a long time to come, though as communication improved and missionaries from the mid-1820s on began to insist on a Christian marriage ceremony the norms of eastern society slowly percolated west and through the ranks.[26]

Although it appears that the rejection of their Indian wives by such "men of station" as Connolly, Simpson and McTavish in the 1830s may be attributed as much to the character of the individuals involved as their social aspirations, this behaviour also revealed the growing importance of adherence to contemporary European norms in Canadian society and the emergence of a complexly stratified society based both on class and ethnic group.

The same qualitative change in attitudes to intermarriage in the West noted in the mid 1820s and encouraged by Simpson and the missionaries — which, it is suggested here, paralleled profound social change in eastern Canada and Britain — was also accompanied by a fundamental change in government policy towards Indians in Upper and Lower Canada.

For most of the eighteenth century Indians in general had been treated with the cautious respect accorded allies in war and partners in trade. After 1812, however, Indians ceased to be regarded as useful allies. In eastern Canada the fur trade was gradually being replaced by agriculture as the main base of the ceremony.[27]

The Indian Department had been a military responsibility since first established in 1755[28] but in 1830 the Upper Canada administration became a civil agency.[29] As Surtees and others have pointed out, this represented an important change in policy, but the personnel in the administration remained the same. Ex-officers and veterans continued to form a large part of the administration.

The administration of the Indian Affairs Department was at first composed entirely of officers appointed as commissioners. As early as 1775, however, an elaborate structure had been put into place with a hierarchy of superintendents, deputy superintendents, agents, interpreters and missionaries. Indian bands were invited to select a spokesman, "a beloved man" to act as their intermediary with the government and important provisions relating to Indian lands, enunciated in the Royal Proclamation of 1763, were amplified. One of these was "that proper measures be taken with the consent and concurrence of the Indians to ascertain and define the precise and exact boundary and limits of the lands which it may be proper to restore to them and where no settlement whatever shall be allowed."[30]

Maintaining the boundaries on Indian lands was by this time an integral part of policy. Also reiterated were the strictures that only the Crown could buy land from Indians and that when purchases were made by the Crown they should be made at "some general meeting at which the principal chiefs of each Tribe claiming a property in such lands are present . . ." The basic formula for treaty-making with Indians was thus established very early on.

Superintendents were given power to "transact all affairs relative to Indians", thus postponing for some time the necessity for legislation for Indians.[31]

Between 1812 and 1830 the change in attitudes appears to have accelerated. Sir George Murray, who took over the Department in 1830, illustrated this change when he commented in a report: "It appears to me that the course which has hitherto been taken in

19

dealing with these people has had reference to the advantages which might be derived from their friendship in time of war rather than to any settled purpose of gradually reclaiming them from a state of barbarism, and of introducing amongst them industrious and peaceful habits of civilized life."[32] This "settled purpose" and all that is implied were to be the basis of future policy for Indians.

In Britain in the early nineteenth century there was a growing interest in social reform in general, the spread of evangelism, and a continuing debate over the abolition of slavery. As a logical extension of these activities a keen interest was also taken in the aboriginal inhabitants of the British colonies. Philanthropic societies, such as the Aborigines Protection Society, consequently produced several reports for their members on the state of the Indians in the North American colonies and continually lobbied the government for better treatment of Indians.[33]

Other reports, triggered by such criticisms, testify to the lack of interest in Indians in the Indian Department in Upper Canada up to 1830. The report, for example, of General Darling stated that Indians were being tricked out of their lands and possessions, that they were destitute and, as an aside, warned that they would soon turn to the Americans if the government didn't help them.[34]

The solution advocated was always the same: a Christian education, permanent settlements and agriculture were the means for bringing the Indians into a state of "civilization" when they would be on a par with other citizens. In the meantime Indians would have to be protected by the Department. But there was then a divergence of opinion on how to proceed. The Indians, it was felt, could be either isolated and then "civilized" or the same objective could be achieved by close interaction with whites of good character. Both approaches were to be experimented with.[35]

Chapter 4

Experimental Approaches 1830-1847

For a time the Indian Department attempted a series of experimental approaches — first at Coldwater and Grassy Narrows Reserve, where the close interaction with white society approach was tried and proved a failure.[1] Then in 1837 the Manitoulin experiment adopted the segregationist approach.[2]

This scheme was largely the brain child of Sir Francis Bond Head, Lieutenant Governor of Upper Canada. Bond Head believed the Indians were "a doomed race melting like snow before the sun."[3] Manitoulin was envisaged by him as a sanctuary where Indians could live out their last days in protective isolation. His reasons for so thinking were, he said, based on the following observations:

> "1) the attempt to make farmers of the Red Men has been, generally speaking, a complete failure.
>
> 2) Congregating them for the purposes of civilization has implanted many more vices than it has eradicated; and consequently 3) the greatest kindness we can perform towards these intelligent simple-minded people is to remove and fortify them as much as possible from all communication with the whites."[4]

Bond Head, however, was no philanthropist. About the same time (in 1836) he obtained over one and a half million acres from the Ottawa and Chippewa Indians paying no compensation at all, as had until then been the custom. Writing to the Colonial Secretary in London he pointed out how economical he had been: "I need hardly observe that I have thus obtained for His Majesty's Government from the Indians an immense portion of most valuable land, which will undoubtedly produce funds more than sufficient to repay the expense of the Indians, and the Indian Department in this Province".[5] But Bond's "Red Children"[6] (as he called them) did not want to move to the rocky and barren island of Manitoulin and preferred to remain where they were. One old chief said, "It is not a good idea to settle too many Indians on that barren rock and I am getting too old and I don't want to go and live like a gull sitting on a rock because that is what sitting on the Manitoulin would be like."[7]

This experiment then also failed. The Indians were proving harder to manipulate (or "guide", as the government saw it) than was at first envisaged. Some new approach was necessary.

A Commission of Inquiry was then set up after 1841 to investigate the condition of the Indians. The report of this Commission is invaluable for the information it provides on attitudes to Indians in general and Indian women in particular, as much as for its content on the situation of the Indians.[8] Information was obtained from questionnaires sent out to the resident Superintendents and the employees of the Indian Department. The questions related to Indians' morals, work habits, agriculture, intermarriage with whites, illegitimacy and so on — the proper concerns of upright British citizens.

The Commissioners were quite candid about their God-given right to Indian lands. At the beginning of their report of 1844-45 they state, "The earth belongs to mankind in general" (i.e., not only to the Indians). "We do not therefore deviate from the views of nature in confining the Indians within narrower limits."[9] The alienation of Indian land, in other words, was part of a law of nature.

The Commissioners recommended as priorities for future Indian policies that Indians should be urged to adopt a settled way of life, Christianity and education of their young by missionaries. It was recommended also that distribution of presents among Indians, which by this time had become an established custom and was a convenient method of census taking, should be gradually discontinued in the interests of economy and the Indians.[10]

On the important question of title deeds for Indians there was some controversy, but the recommendation went forward. Earlier in 1837 Peter Jones, a missionary, had written to Lord Glenlea, "So long as they hold no written document from the British government to show that the land is theirs, they fear that the white man may at some future day take their lands away from them."[11] The point would seem to have been taken that Indians didn't trust the government any more than they trusted the settlers.

The Commissioners admitted on looking back, as so many future Commissions were to do, "the error of past government and its evil consequences."[12] Nevertheless, despite "the errors of government" and the pessimism of Bond Head (and his successor Sydenham, who held similarly apocalyptic views), the Commissioners optimistically felt that in both Upper and Lower Canada, the Indians had "attained the same stage of civilization at which their further progress requires more enlarged measures, and more active interference."

The report also includes revealing comments which demonstrate a complete lack of understanding of the customs of the Indians of Upper and Lower Canada. An Indian was "docile", "happy" and "hospitable" naturally, but "in his half-civilized state he is indolent to excess, intemperate, suspicious, cunning, covetous and addicted to lying and fraud." Since this stereotype applied to all Indians, they had a lot of work ahead of them. Among the Indians of Lower Canada they found it noteworthy that "the birth of illegitimate children is less frequent than formerly, but an event of this nature does not cast a stigma upon the mother; nor upon the child, which is usually adopted into the tribe". They also reported that women were still the providers: "One of the peculiarities of Indians in their native state is their proud aversion to labour; hence in the early stages of civilization they are accustomed to impose upon the women the greater part of the labour in the field and household. This continues to prevail among the Indians."

Yet further on they explained that each worked his own parcel although the land was communally held. They stated: "He cultivates (his parcel) for the support of his own family, without interference, and secure from the intrusion of his neighbours. This parcel he can bequeath to his heirs, etc." What is evident here is that "Indian" in their minds refers to a male only.

The Commissioners, relying on written reports, are unlikely to have known much about the traditions of the Indians and so the explanation for the women doing most of the work had to be that it was an aberration and the result of male "indolence". The male remained nevertheless in their minds the "titular" worker and owner. This is important when the later legislation is considered.

They were particularly pleased with the advancement of the Indians of Caughnawaga. "There is scarcely a pure blooded Indian in the settlement", they noted, and also that there had been fewer illegitimate births. Where a family had no land the men worked on boats and rafts in the summer and the women made baskets, snowshoes and moccasins.

Among the Algonquian, Nipissings and Iroquois at the Lake of Two Mountains in general, "The greater part of the field labour is performed by the women, assisted by their husbands." The first two, however, still led a roving life and only the women and aged men farmed small patches, whereas the Iroquois farmed more extensively. Lumber operations had destroyed or scared away the game and in general, the commissioners noted, "They are much less well off than they were forty years before."

An important indication of the operation of a class/caste system is evident in this report from Caughnawaga to the same Commission: "The Superintendent stated that he considers these Indians to be very little inferior to the lower order of the French Canadian population in the District". In other words, the Indians' position was seen, at least by those who controlled a large part of their lives, as part of a hierarchical ordering of class and race.

The Commissioners concluded finally that the Indians continued "to require special protection and guidance of the Government". There was clearly no contradiction in the minds of the Commissioners. What is crucial here is that this mid-nineteenth century perception of "protection" and "guidance" constituted the ideological underpinnings of subsequent legislation in the nineteenth century. The "protection" afforded the Indians was highly ambiguous but not inconsistent with the logic of the time.

What emerged then from this report was not really a recommendation for a change in policy, but rather an expression of hardening attitudes. In summary, Indians were believed to be amenable to civilization, but it would take a little longer than originally thought and stricter laws, and more "interference" was necessary. Indians had no right, natural or otherwise, to land which God had meant for everyone, and therefore restrictions on their territories were in accordance with the laws of nature. Indians weren't ready for civil rights, but such rights should be held out as an incentive to "progress".

Whether this attitude may be characterized as protective is surely debatable. Certainly the equation, juxtaposition and constant reiteration of the terms "paternalism", "protection" and "welfare" of the Indians have been a convenient smoke screen for all Canadian governments, and have long served to confuse the issue.

Chapter 5

Acts for Indians 1850-1867

The report of the Commission of Inquiry in 1847 prompted two Acts for Indians — one in Lower Canada, another in Upper Canada. Indians in Lower Canada (Quebec) had not been allocated reserves in the same way as those of Upper Canada (Ontario). Fixed lands had been granted to the Jesuits for reserves under their aegis by the Ancien Régime. In 1851, 230,000 additional acres of land were therefore allotted to Indians in Lower Canada "from motives of compassion".[1]

In 1850, reflecting perhaps the problem this land grant was meant to solve, a mechanism was set in place to determine who should have the right to live on Indian lands in Lower Canada.

This Act included the first statutory definition of who was an Indian — "An Act for the better protection of the Lands and Property of the Indians in Lower Canada". The relevant section of the Act reads:

"V. And for the purpose of determining any right of property, possession or occupation in or to any lands . . . the following classes of persons are and shall be considered as Indians . . .

First — All persons of Indian Blood, reputed to belong to the particular Body or Tribe of Indians interested in such lands, and their descendants.

Secondly — All persons intermarried with such Indians and residing amongst them, and the descendants of all such persons.

Thirdly — All persons residing among such Indians, whose parents on either side were or are Indians of such Body or Tribe, or entitled to be considered as such; And

Fourthly — All persons adopted in infancy by any such Indians, etc."[2]

This very broad definition was amended one year later and made slightly more restrictive. The second section — "all persons intermarried with such Indians" — was deleted, as was the section on adoption. A new section was added, permitting women who married non-Indians and their descendants to be considered Indians but excluding the non-Indian spouses of Indian women from this privilege. Indian status thus depended on Indian descent or marriage to a male Indian.[3]

In Upper Canada, on the other hand, a companion act of 1850

was entitled "An Act for the protection of the Indians in Upper Canada from imposition, and the property occupied or enjoyed by them from trespass and injury". The definition of an Indian in this Act consisted only of the statement that the Act applied to "Indians, and those who may be inter-married with Indians".[4]

A number of provisions in this Act had the consequence of making an Indian a minor at law — for example, the inability to be bonded or held responsible "for any contract whatsoever". Among other noteworthy provisions were the exception from taxation, and punishment for trespass on reserves for all "except Indians and those who may be inter-married with Indians". Presents and annuities were to be continued, though this had long been a controversial issue and efforts were continually being made to reduce the costs of the Indian Department. Indeed, in 1854, Oliphant, Superintendent of Indian Affairs, in a report to Lord Elgin recommended the reduction of the Indian Department.[5] His successor, Viscount Bury, wrote to Sir Edmund Head one year later rejecting Oliphant's scheme, pointing out the "burdens which the withdrawal of all primary assistance would entail upon the Indians".[6]

Sir Edmund Head, (a relative of Sir Edmund Bond Head) Governor of Canada after Elgin, summed up the inherent contradiction in the situation in a letter to Labouchère in the Colonial Office: "I approach the whole subject with pain and misgiving because I never feel quite confident of reconciling the perfect good faith of England towards the Aborigines with the national wish of the Queen's Government to effect the abolition of all charge on the Imperial revenue; a course which I know to be in the abstract, right and desirable in every way."[7]

Labouchère, however, made the limited extent of Department sympathy quite clear in his reply: "It has long been settled that the general presents to the Indian tribes which are in progress of annual reduction shall cease in 1858 ... This decision will therefore remain unaltered."[8]

Attitudes in Canada were hardening in proportion to the increasing pressures of European settlement. The problems of the Indians were beginning to be viewed more and more as the result not of depredations on their land by Europeans but of Indian improvidence and lack of "progress".

In 1857 "an Act to encourage the gradual Civilization of the Indian Tribes in the Province, and to amend the Laws respecting Indians"[9] was made applicable to both Canadas. The title clearly expresses its intent to expedite the process of "civilizing" the Indians through offering incentives to them to enfranchise. Enfranchisement was seen as a mechanism "to facilitate the acquisition of property and of rights accompanying it, by such Individual Members of the said Tribes as shall be found to deserve such encouragement and to have deserved it."[10] Ownership of property was the prerequisite for civil rights and responsibilities which were by definition indivisible from civilization.

Thus enfranchisement, that "quaint piece of legal Canadiana" as one writer has called it, first appeared in legislation, offering as inducements land in fee simple and a lump sum payment of a share of annuities and band funds.[11] Only males could be enfranchised, dependents being enfranchised with the male.

The definition of Indian in this Act for both Upper and Lower Canada was not that of the earlier Lower Canada Act, but the more inclusive designation of the Upper Canada Act: Indians or persons of "Indian blood or intermarried with Indians."[12]

At the same time, yet another Commission of Inquiry was established with very similar terms of reference to those which had been given the commissioners ten years earlier. They were to recommend:

"1st   As to the best means of securing the future progress and civilization of the Indian Tribes in Canada.

2nd   As to the best mode of so managing the Indian property as to receive its full benefits to the Indians."[13]

In other words, it was accepted that the settlement of the country could only be accomplished by taking over Indian lands. The question was how best to manage this so as to protect the interests of all concerned. In addition, a positive secular programme emphasizing the benefits of civilizaton was to be initiated, encouraging Indians to give up their ties to their bands and accept in recompense property in fee simple, the sine qua non of citizenship.

Civilizing and good management then were still primary, but the report acknowledged that earlier experiments had been unsuccessful. The Commissioners concluded, "We consider that it may be fairly assumed to be established that there is no inherent defect in the organization of the Indians, which disqualifies them from being reclaimed from their savage state". But civilization for the Indians was still "but a glimmering and distant spark".[14]

Their report of 1858 contained two recommendations of interest here and which give some further insight into the mood of the times. The first relates to Indian lands, which the Commissioners believed were too large for the number of Indians occupying them. They therefore recommended that legislation be enacted obliging Indians in future, when reserves were being designated, to accept a lot of a maximum of 25 acres per family.[15]

In addition, "the gradual destruction of the tribal organization" was recommended and its substitution with a municipal form of government.[16]

However, subsequent legislation prior to Confederation did not contain these or any substantially new provisions. But these recommendations were not forgotten, and it will be seen that virtually all subsequent legislation for Indians had three main functions:

1) "Civilizing" the Indians — that is, assimilating them (and their lands) into the Euro-Canadian citizenry;
2) While accomplishing this, the ever more efficient "better management" of Indians and their lands was always a goal to be striven for and, following on this, an important element in better management was controlling expenditure and resources;
3) To accomplish this efficiently it became important to define who was an Indian and who was not.

Yet the British North America Act (B.N.A. Act) of 1867, "an Act for the Union of Canada, Nova Scotia, and New Brunswick, and the Government thereof; and for Purposes connected therewith", contains only seven words relating to Indians. In section 91, which gives exclusive legislative authority to Parliament for some 29 items, "Indians, and lands reserved for the Indians" is number 24 in the list, between "Copyrights" and "Naturalization and Aliens".[17]

A great deal depends on the interpretation of these seven words and the argument has been made by Kenneth Lysyk and Cumming and Mickenberg (among others) that the Indian Act "cannot affect a person's status as an Indian under the the terms of the B.N.A. Act" and that aboriginal rights cannot be affected by exclusion from the Indian Act (Inuit for example are excluded from the Indian Act) since "these rights flow from an individual's status as a 'native person' and his connection with a particular tribe (in the case of Indians) rather than from any provision of the Indian Act".[18] By this argument an Indian woman who has been subject to involuntary enfranchisement remains an Indian in law.

There is as yet, however, no definition of who is a "native person" in Canadian law who might therefore also be an "Indian" by aboriginal right under the B.N.A. Act.

28

Chapter 6

Better Management, 1868-1869

One year after Confederation, in 1868, "An Act providing for the organization of the Department of Secretary of State of Canada, and for the management of Indian and Ordinance Lands" consolidated previous legislation and retained virtually unchanged in section 15 the broad 1851 Lower Canada provisions regarding who was an Indian for the purposes of the legislation.[1]

One year later, in 1869, however, another Act unambiguously aimed at "better management" and tighter controls contained far-reaching changes. It was entitled "An Act for the gradual enfranchisement of Indians, the better management of Indian Affairs and to extend the provisions of Act 31st Victoria Chapter 42" (i.e., the 1868 Act).[2] The Superintendent General of Indian Affairs (or his agent) was given very wide powers. He had the right to determine who could use Indian lands and there was a concomitant emphasis put on the holding of a licence or location ticket which indicated the right to hold a particular plot of land. He had the power to stop or divert Indian funds and annuities. Less than one-quarter Indian blood was to be a disqualification for "annuity interest or rent". Those "intermarried with Indians settling on these lands ... without licence" were liable to be "summarily ejected". Prison terms were to be levied as well as the fines prescribed in the previous Acts for supplying liquor to Indians.

On the death of an Indian his "goods and chattels" and land rights were to be passed to his children. The wife was excluded, her maintenance being the responsibility of the children.

A council was to be elected by the "male members of each Indian Settlement of the full age of twenty-one years at such time and place and in such manner as the Superintendent General may direct." They might, however, be removed by the Governor for "dishonesty, intemperance or immorality."

If an Indian was enfranchised his wife and minor children were also automatically enfranchised.

Most significant in this paper, however, is the following amendment in section 6 concerning Indian women marrying non-Indians or Indians from other bands. "Provided always that any Indian woman marrying any other than an Indian shall cease to be an Indian within the meaning of this Act, nor shall the children issue of such a marriage be considered as Indians within the meaning of this Act." On marrying an Indian from another tribe, band or body, she and their children "belong to their father's tribe only."

The Indian woman was here for the first time given fewer rights in law than an Indian man. She could not vote in band elections. She could not inherit from her husband. She could not marry out of her band without penalty. Particularly punitive was the introduction of the proviso that she and her children would lose forever their Indian rights if she married a non-Indian and the possibility that she might then be obliged to leave the reserve since her husband could be "summarily ejected" at the order of the superintendent.

Section 4, however, seemed to allow a loophole allowing such women and children annuities in that it stated only that less than one-quarter Indian blood was a disentitlement to annuities. Since the Act also stated that the Indian woman marrying out "ceased to be an Indian" this was clearly ambiguous.

Section 6 of the 1869 Act, which decreed that female Indians were no longer Indians on "marrying out", was subsequently much elaborated upon. It proved to be a source of great bitterness and divisiveness among Indians and extremely difficult to administer. Nevertheless, it has not only remained firmly embedded in the Act right down to the present day but, with its numerous refinements and embellishments, it is far more restrictive than was ever envisaged even in its Victorian heyday. It therefore seems crucial here to attempt to determine if possible the rationale behind the introduction of Section 6 into the 1869 Act.

In the Lavell case of 1973, for example, the argument was advanced that this legislative enactment was devised to protect Indians and their lands, and it would seem that this argument is believed by many to carry some weight. However, there is very little in previous legislation or in such documents as the reports of special commissions to indicate that this was ever more than a very limited and qualified intention, even then the protection which was envisaged was based on assumptions (such as those embodied in the Commission of 1858 recommendations) which consciously set out to eliminate those things which Indians most prized — their communally held lands and 'tribal' way of life.

The Indians themselves objected strenuously to penalties being imposed on Indian women but were ignored. In 1872 the Grand Council of Ontario and Quebec Indians (founded in 1870) sent a strong letter to the Minister at Ottawa protesting among other things section 6 of the 1869 Act in the following unmistakable terms: "They [the members of the Grand Council] also desire amendments to Section 6 of the Act of 1869 so that Indian women may have the privilege of marrying when and whom they please; without subjecting themselves to exclusion or expulsion from their tribes and the consequent loss of property and the rights they may have by virtue of their being members of any particular tribe."[3] The Indians' request went unheeded.

The legislation can only be understood in the social and political context of the time.

In the new Dominion of Canada only two years after Confederation there could be no blueprint for the future, but there were three clear goals, none of which could be accomplished without first displacing Indians or Métis. First, to create a united Canada coast to coast, to settle the West as quickly as possible with loyal citizens, and to both accomplish and consolidate this by means of a fast and efficient trans-Canada railway system. The ever present threat of American expansion north made this obligatory, according to historian Morris Zaslow, who comments:

> "The American westward movement, particularly after 1850 ... made it imperative for British North Americans to match this advance by expanding west into the territories of the British Crown. Not to do so would expose those lands to the danger of being overwhelmed by the United States and would condemn the people of Canada to their present narrow limits and to a lower standard of living than their neighbours. Expansion became a national duty for Canada, a commitment with destiny."[4]

Hector Langevin, the Minister responsible for Indian Affairs in 1869, introduced the Bill in the House of Commons and stressed that its aim was to make enfranchisement less difficult, that an Indian "by his education, good conduct and intelligence would be granted a lot on a reserve which would be held by him and then his children in fee simple. This was another attempt in the direction of civilizing the Indians, and the government should try as much as possible to protect them in the first entrance," he said.[5]

Very important here though is the rationale relating to the introduction of section 6 which stated that Indian women marrying non-Indians ceased to be Indians. To get the full flavour it is necessary to quote this portion of his speech in full.

> "Again, it was found that in many tribes there was a want of proper discrimination between those who belonged to the tribe and those who came on the reserve from some other quarter. Many came in on the plea of being Indians and divided the revenues of the tribe, which, of course, impoverished them and deprived them of the means of maintaining their families. This Bill provided that, when an Indian woman married a white, as regarded her rights to the reserve, her children would not be considered Indians, but would assume the position of the father. So also an Indian woman of one tribe marrying a member of another tribe became a member of her husband's tribe. Again it has been found with reference to reserves that a good many Indians took advantage of the weakness of others and took possession of more land than they had the right to have ... By this Bill it was provided that no Indian would be recognized as having a right to any land unless he received a location from the Superintendent of Indian Affairs. Again, the complaint was often brought against the

31

Indians that they did not keep up their roads, bridges, fences and ditches. In this Bill authority was given to compel the chiefs to have their roads, etc., kept in proper order. If they failed to do so the Superintendent would provide for the work being done at the cost of the tribe."[6]

The intent of the Act is here abundantly clear — more control over Indians, more efficient and thus more economical management of Indian affairs during the transition to civilization and eventual assimilation. In the meantime Indians had to be taught "proper discrimination" of who could come on their reserves. Sharing with visiting or indigent Indians was unwise and would lead to want for all and must be discouraged. Significantly, few words are spared to explain Section 6, which deprives the Indian woman of her status. But this and the succeeding sentence, stating that an Indian woman marrying an Indian from another tribe becomes a member of her husband's tribe, follow immediately on the previous one emphasizing "proper discrimination" and the necessity for alleviating financial burdens on the reserve. Making half-Indian children no longer Indians was part of this same logic.

Indians as problems — not problems of Indians — is the tenor of the proposed Act and this is further clarified in the questions posed in the subsequent debate.

The first question in the debate came from Mr. Holton who, after describing the general provisions as "well considered", went on: "We understood the honourable gentleman to say that a white man married to an Indian would be expelled from the reserve. This could cause great hardship if applied retroactively." He asked what special provisions had been made for such cases. He made these remarks, he said, "with special reference to the Caughnawaga Reserve, in which people of the County (Chateauguay) he had the honour to represent took a very warm interest."[7]

Hector Langevin replied it was the wish of the Government to apply the rule referred to by the member for Chateauguay "only to the case of white men as misbehaved for selling liquor, or robbing the Indians of their timber . . . As regards those who were married to Indian women, and there was nothing alleged against their conduct, they received a licence to remain."[8]

This exchange, though rather confused, does indicate that the intent was not to penalize the white man who could continue to live on the reserve with his Indian wife. The expressed intent was to prevent their children, "half-breeds", from having any rights to live on the reserve.

Another member of the House, Mr. Dorion, said that he thought it was the duty of the government to try to encourage intermarriage between whites and Indians, not to discourage it. He believed it would tend to raise the character of the whole tribe. Ordinary tribunals, he believed, could deal with white men who sold liquor, etc. Mr. Langevin answered this by saying that he had been misunderstood. The govern-

ment would not and could not discourage marriage between Indians and whites and, he said, "As soon as the title of land was given to the Indians they would be in the same position on it as whites."[9]

It was other Indians who were mentioned as taking lands from Indians, and the effect on the Indian woman of section 6 was not even mentioned — "As regards her rights to the reserve her children would not be considered Indians."[10] Also, as Langevin implied in his answer to Dorion, it was envisaged that the reserves would eventually be broken up into lots held in fee simple as all Indians were enfranchised and thus assimilated. As Langevin explained, it would make no difference in the long run. Section 6 was clearly not meant as a mechanism for protecting Indians from whites.

Judging from these remarks in the House, section 6 was nothing more than a muddled attempt to achieve the greater efficiency and the easier management of budgets that it was hoped would occur when the number of Indians to be dealt with didn't keep fluctuating. There is no "malice aforethought" — in fact not too much forethought about possible side effects at all. Was it then, like much of the legislation for Indians, nothing more than a piece of ill-considered "adhoc-ery"?[11] Were Langevin and his administrators unaware of the injurious effects of this legislation on Indian women?

More conclusive evidence on this is contained in an important paper prepared by an anthropologist, Sally Weaver, for the opposition to Lavell and Bedard in the Lavell case. Weaver's conclusion is that "If the question is asked — 'Why did the Canadian Government in 1869 legislate against the Indian woman retaining her status as Indian if she married a whiteman?' — the answer is clearly — to protect Indian land from both the occupation and use of it by whitemen married to Indian women."[12] But Langevin denied this in the House and white men continued to live on the reserves with the protection of the Department.

The documents cited by Professor Weaver in fact lend support to what are somewhat different conclusions. It is necessary however to examine these documents in some detail before this can become clear.

First of all Weaver's data show that Indians themselves were not necessarily interested or willing parties to striking women off the band registers. It would appear also that the Superintendent of Indian Affairs, Hector Langevin, the Deputy Superintendent of Indian Affairs, William Sprague, and Jasper Gilkinson, the Visiting Superintendent to the Six Nations (the main emphasis of Weaver's research was with reference to the Six Nations) had clearly had the final if not the first word in controlling band business. Also when it came to penalizing Indian females on intermarriage (and it becomes clear that such a policy was being pursued) they went so far as to assure the doubting Indians on every possible occasion that such behaviour was "customary". A letter from Hector Langevin in 1867 (two years before the legislation was even enacted) to the Chippewa Indian woman Sahga-mah-qua and her daughters illustrates this point:

> "In replying to your petition, applying for land with the Chippewas of Muncey Town in the Township of Caradoc, these remarks are made for your guidance and information. The rule appears to have been followed, and I think correctly among Indian Bands, that upon any Indian Woman marrying out from her people, she ceases to belong to them, and if her husband belonged to another Indian Band, she became a member of his Band. The same principle should prevail if she married a White Man — but as she in such a case could not elsewhere be put upon a pay list for Interest and annuity money, she should continue to receive her usual portion and her Children would likewise be entitled to shares — As to land the case is different. The Father being a White Man could have no right to Indian land, and Indian Women have only such right in land belonging to their Tribes, as they enjoy jointly with their Husbands."[13]

The 1868 Act nevertheless did not take away the Indian women's rights to hold property on the reserve but it is evident from this letter that such a policy was being pursued up to the enactment of the legislation in 1869 which did take away land rights for the first time from women who "married out."

The vital role played by the Superintendent in explaining the "custom" as well as the drive for more control is again emphasized in this rather different item from the minutes of February 7th, 1871.

> "The Supt, said, this was just a case where he had to exercise his opinion, and for the reasons, that it would be a departure from the rule and usage so long respected and recognized. In this instance, was the fact, that Martin had some years ago sold out his possessions and bid good bye to his people, and went away to the Saugeen, and now, he does not say he will return, only desires they may be again added to the roll of the Six Nations. Therefore, he could not consent to place him or his family on the list."[14]

Weaver, in an appendix, notes that the influence of the Superintendent David Thorburn was "frequently obvious" in 1858 when decisions were being arrived at on annuities. For example if a family was away for a long time and wished to have their names re-entered on the pay list he suggested that they should first have to prove themselves of "good character and worth, to be members".[15]

Superintendent Thorburn's perception of his role as instructor on not only custom but morals is quite clear in this excerpt from Weaver's report:

> "A year later, David Thorburn in writing to R. L. Pennefather, Superintendent General of Indian Affairs (1856-1861) provides the following information on what appear to be Departmental principles which have
themselves of "good character and worth, to be members."[15]

> "It's a definite rule for striking off absent members of a Band or Tribe. The practice is, and has been, when any member absents him or herself voluntarily, whether to a distance or to a foreign country without the Consent or Knowledge of the Band or Tribe, they are not entitled to the benefits that resident individuals are, because they share no part of the Common burdens, such as road labor, or aiding in clearing up the lands in the Settlement again. Besides we know not what their behavior may have been while so absent. There is also a practice any convicted of Crime in the Penitentiary, no allowance while so confined, or for extreme bad behaviour by setting a bad example by bringing the Tribes into discredit by word or deed. If absent in a foreign country, we can have no knowledge what they have been doing or even a distance in the Province they not infrequently join other bands and with them participate of the common benefits of the Band — the Foregoing principles have been inculcated from time to time from the head of the Department, and acted on by me. If you approve of the points laid down, or some other, it would be well to embody them into a Circular for a guide."[16]

Again citing from notes from Six Nations Band Records Weaver writes:

> "In the Council Minutes of January 20, 1870 a difference of opinion between the chiefs and the Superintendent reflects the council's opinion of the 1869 Act.

> "The Speaker rose and said, they did not concur in erasing this

young woman, as they had not been consulted in framing the Act passed in Parliament, and they refused to recognize it, and therefore, would retain the young woman on the list. They intended to represent their views. The Supt. pointed out, that whatever might be their objections to the Act, it was clear the clause 6 is based upon the usage and customs of the Indian tribes, and often, had the Council denounced the admission of Whitemen upon their lands, and called upon him, The Supt. to expel them."[17]

It is quite clear from this that the Indians of the Six Nations of Ontario differentiated between the depredations of undesirable white men on the reserve and penalizing Indian women.

That the Indians in Caughnawaga in Quebec were concerned and puzzled is again evident in the following letter from Hector Langevin to Sawatis Anionkui, Peter Karenho and other Iroquois Indians at Caughnawaga.

"With reference to your Memorial of the 4th May last I have to inform you that the Act regarding Indian Affairs passed in the Year 1868 continues in force and the Act passed during the last Session of Parliament of which a Copy is enclosed does not change the Act of 1868 in any way injurious to the interest of the Indians but on the contrary by Section No. 6 it provides for excluding in future any Woman of Indian Blood who marries after the passing of this Act a man of other origin or of another Tribe or Band from continuing a Member of that Tribe or Band to which she originally belonged. Thus preventing men not of Indian Blood having by marrying Indian women either through their Wives or Children any pretext for Settling on Indian lands."[18]

The fact that Indian women were being injured was just not germane to the issue.

The documents cited in Weaver's report also underline the moral judgements which underlay decisions and how they would be applied differently to males and females. Consider for example the following remark about an Indian woman Lucinda Scott in a letter from Hector Langevin to Gilkison of August 1869, "as it appears that some two or three years since she became married to the white man George Scott and thus made the best amends in her power for her past misconduct, etc. . . ."[19]

William Sprague, Deputy Superintendent of Indian Affairs, in the Annual Report of 1870 explains the legislation of 1868 as, among other things, part of a concerted effort to guide Indians into realizing the value of holding private property. As indicated by Hector Langevin the necessity was to restrain *Indians* from "trafficking one with another" so that one or two do not end up with "two or three times as much as the proper quota".[20] Sprague also lamented the lack of laws restraining Indians from letting their lands to others to farm, which he believed "has induced the tendency to indolence and its concomitant misfortunes observable among so many of Indian blood."[21] Much the same sentiment was expressed twenty years before by the 1844-45 Report of the Investigative Commission.

Sprague seems also to be concerned on another score; that of categorizing Indians according to blood or colour and keeping the race "pure". "But it is becoming more and more perceptable that the Law should define the point beyond which persons of mixed Indian and white blood should not be regarded as Indians. I think that in justice to the Indian people with more than one fourth white blood should not be regarded as Indians but as belonging to the race giving them their predominating color."[22] This would mean presumably that the children of anyone male or female who married out would lose Indian status and that the "blood" of both Indians and whites would become more "pure" with time.

What is most evident, in summary, is that there was little consistency in the administration of Indian Affairs in Upper Canada and Lower Canada and a great deal of latitude allowed for individual officials to implement their own moral convictions and that this had been the case for quite a long time. According to a memo of 1872 from Sprague to Joseph Howe, Langevin's successor, women from the Mississaugas of Alnwick who "married out" had been excluded from the paylist, i.e., had not received annuities for 40 years (since 1832).[23] And Indians then had also protested furiously.

In 1860, according to the transactions of the Aborigines Protection Society, Mrs. Catherine Sutton, Nah-ne-Bah-Nee-Quay, an Indian woman, was so outraged at being refused her annuity that she went to London to complain and obtained an audience with Queen Victoria at Buckingham Palace. As a result she was permitted to purchase the land on which she and her family had been living.[24]

Communications between the Indians and Ottawa were usually channelled through the Agent — a department employee. If the Agent did not give his approval and assistance Indians were clearly at a disadvantage in registering complaints with Ottawa. It was thus rather difficult for Indians who perceived legal injustices to make their complaints heard and also keep abreast of the changes in the law when they had to depend on the government Agent for all information. The Agent was also in a difficult position since he was in a conflict of interest and unable to represent fairly the interests of his clients, the Indians, in complaints against his employer, the government.

As well, agents themselves were often unclear as to specific government policies and even less able to understand their rationale. In June 1869 for example George Cherrier, the agent from Caughnawaga, sent a letter to Ottawa requesting instruction on the new legislation and including a list of all the white men on Caughnawaga, twenty-eight names in all. The reply was quite brusque in tone stating that: "White men married to Indian women prior to the passing of the Act V32-33C6 (S.6) are privileged to reside on Reserves and Indian widows have received permission to allow white men to work their farms, etc." In fact all but two of the men named had a licence to live on the reserve. Many of the names have Indian names pencilled beside them (Indian wives' names possibly). The two men without licences were Giroux, the tavern keeper, and Hébert, "a good blacksmith".[25]

On the effects of section 6 Agent Cherrier commented in 1872, "the practical effect is to promote immorality . . . An Indian widow with property cohabited with a white and the only bar to their marriage was the fact that the moment she married she would cease to be a member of the band and consequently lose her rights as an Indian and be subject to immediate eviction from the property left her by her husband." Cherrier advised the government to accede to the request of 1872 of the Indian Council "in order to allay suspicions or apprehensions . . . as to the intentions of the Government with respect to them."[26]

It is evident that even if the Indians of Ontario and Quebec did not like white men on the reserves they certainly did not approve of the government remedy and that they saw this as an attack not only on female Indians but on all Indians.

In conclusion it is clear that although Langevin was himself rather inconsistent, he shared with Sprague and their colleagues three deeply held convictions and that the statutes of 1869 and section 6 in particular embodied these principles:

1) Indians and their lands were to be assimilated. The number of Indians was to be gradually reduced. This was the final solution envisaged by everyone except the Indians and long term protection of Indian lands was logically inconsistent with this view.

2) Indians were not capable of making rational decisions for their own welfare and this had to be done by the Department on their behalf. Though Indians believed their welfare depended on their retaining as much of their lands as possible, the attainment of government goals depended on alienating Indian lands.

3) Indian women should be subject to their husbands as were other women. Their children were his children alone in law. It was inconceivable that an Indian woman should be able to own and transmit property and rights to her children.

Chapter 7

Homes and Gardens, 1870-1874

Indian legislation after 1869 became increasingly restrictive as government policies toward the Indian people were developed. The attitudes of the Indians themselves to half-breeds and to Indian-white relations are indicated in the negotiations for the numbered treaties which were made from 1871 on.

Government policy was typified in the comment of Lieutenant-Governor Morris in "The Treaties of Canada with the Indians of Manitoba and the North-West Territories." "I had ascertained that the Indian mind was oppressed with vague fears; they dreaded the treaty; they had been made to believe that they would be compelled to live on the reserves . . . and abandon their hunting. . . . I impressed on them the necessity of changing their present mode of life, and commencing to make homes and gardens for themselves."[1]

Treaties were not made with all Indians in Canada. Large areas of British Columbia, the Yukon, the Northwest Territories and Quebec have never been surrendered by treaty. "Treaty Rights" or the benefits guaranteed in treaties to Indians in return for giving up their land for settlement is therefore an incorrect and confusing term to use in referring to all registered Indians' legal rights. Since all registered Indians whether they took treaty or not come under the Indian Act, most of the benefits guaranteed in treaties have been extended to all. There are however some differences in the benefits accorded treaty Indians and other Indians — the major one is that "annuities", which are small sums of money paid annually to each member of the bands who took treaty, are not paid to non-treaty Indians. These sums range from $4 to $5 per person per annum (more for a chief).[2]

In 1870, before the first numbered treaty in 1871 was concluded, the very important transfer of the Hudson's Bay Company Territories to the Dominion of Canada was finally accomplished.[3]

The province of Manitoba was formed and the government immediately issued instructions to the Lieutenant-Governor of the Northwest Territories. "You will also turn your attention promptly to the condition of the country outside of the Province of Manitoba, on the North and West; and while assuring the Indians of your desire to establish friendly relations with them, you will ascertain and report to His Excellency the course you may think the most advisable to pursue whether by Treaty or otherwise, for the removal of any obstructions that might be presented to the flow of population into the fertile lands that be between Manitoba and the Rocky Mountains."[4]

Incentives to rapid settlement came with the Dominion Lands Act of 1872 which promised 160 acres of free land to anyone who would go West.[5] A few years later an amendment to the Act permitted white women also to obtain a free homestead. Indians were excluded from Homestead Acts.[6] In the Treaties after 1870 a male Indian was allotted about 160 acres per family of five on a reserve.[7]

The treaty making which now commenced in the West was seen as a matter of the greatest urgency. Prior to Confederation one hundred and twenty-three Treaties and land surrenders had already been signed with the Indians of Eastern Canada and these had established a pattern for treaty-making.[8] From 1871-1876 seven Treaties were negotiated which ceded to the Crown almost the whole of the fertile Prairie region.[9]

In the new Province of Manitoba land grants of 160 acres, or scrip valued at $160, were also offered to the Métis (Half-breeds) in recognition and extinguishment of their aboriginal title.[10] This concession on the part of the Government was clearly a result of the pressure from the Métis leader Louis Riel and his followers in 1869.[11]

Those who lived with Indians but accepted this land grant by so doing were considered by the government to have made themselves ineligible to live on a reserve. Many half-breeds, however, chose not to accept a land grant or scrip and their names were put on Treaty lists. Many were left without either scrip or treaty rights.[12]

Indians in the Prairie regions in the 1870's were already aware that the buffalo, on which they depended for existence, were disappearing and that their living conditions were deteriorating. Over the border in the United States the example of the Battle of Little Big Horn in 1876 (and later Wounded Knee in 1890) was a constant reminder of the price of resistance. It must have seemed that to try to prevent the advance of "civilization" was a futile endeavour and the only thing left for Indians to do was try to make as good a bargain as possible in the short time left. But if they had any hesitation about taking treaty and wanted to retain more land than they were being allocated, as when Treaty No. I was being negotiated, they were given short shrift. On this Lieutenant Governor Archibald wrote to the Secretary of State, Joseph Howe, "We heard them out, and then told them [the Indians] it was quite clear that they had entirely misunderstood the meaning and intention of reserves. . . . We . . . told them it was of no use for them to entertain any such ideas, which were entirely out of the question. We told them that whether they wished it or not, immigrants would come in and fill up the country; that every year from this one twice as many in number as their whole people there assembled would pour into the Province, and in a little while would spread all over it, and that now was the time for them to come to an arrangement that would secure homes and annuities for themselves and their children."[13] There was no mistaking this crude threat and Archibald ends his letter "The observations seemed to command the acquiescence of the majority . . ."[14]

Nevertheless the Indians negotiating Treaty no. I did attempt to bargain not only for themselves but for the half-breeds who were the progeny of the Indian-white marriages, discussed earlier in this paper, when the amount of the annuities was agreed on ($12 per family of five) and then was being paid. Lieutenant Governor Simpson, who as Indian Commissioner negotiated Treaties I and II, provides this interesting commentary on the procedure:

> "A number of those residing among the Indians, and calling themselves Indians, are in reality half-breeds and entitled to share in the land-grant under the provisions of the Manitoba Act . . . The matter as it affected himself (the half-breed) and his children was explained to him, *and the choice given to him to characterize himself.* A very few only decided upon taking their grants as half-breeds. The explanation of this apparent sacrifice is found in the fact that most of these persons have lived all their lives on the Indian reserves (so-called) . . ."[15]

Simpson at any rate seems to have accepted that this was their business and not his.

But Lieutenant Governor Morris, who negotiated the subsequent treaties, took the conventional European stand on how membership should be decided. In his own account of the negotiations he describes his exchange with an Indian Chief while negotiating Treaty No. III.

> "CHIEF — "I should not feel happy if I was not to mess with some of my children that are around me — those children that we call the Half-breed — those that have been born of our women of Indian Blood. We wish that they be counted with us, and have their share of what you have promised. We wish you to accept our demands. It is the Half-breeds that are actually living amongst us — those that are married to our women.
>
> "GOVERNOR — "I am sent here to treat with the Indians. In Red River where I come from, and where there is a great body of Half-breeds, they must be either white or Indian. If Indians they get treaty money; if the Half-breeds call themselves white, they get land. All I can do is refer the matter to the government at Ottawa, and recommend what you wish to be granted.
>
> "CHIEF — "I hope you will not drop the question. We have understood you to say that you came here as a friend . . . You must remember that our hearts and our brains are like paper; we never forget."[16]

This exchange illustrates much the same point as was made earlier here — the imposition on the Indian families and bands of categories and racial divisions which were against the expressed desire of the Indians and contrary to their perception of band affiliation.

In the making of Treaty No. IV the Indians wanted to make the point clear that Half-breeds were kinsmen, and (again quoting from Morris' records) we have the following interesting exchange:

"THE GAMBLER the [Indian spokesman] — ". . . Now when you [Morris] have come here you see sitting out there a mixture of Half-breeds, Crees, Saulteux and Stonies, all are one, and you were slow in taking the hand of a Half-breed. All these things are many things that are in my way. I cannot speak about them.

"LIEUT.-GOV. MORRIS — "I do not quite understand another point. We have here Crees, Saulteux, Assiniboines and other Indians, they are all one, and we have another people, the Half-breeds, that are of your own blood and my blood . . . There was a Half-breed came forward to the table. He was only one of many here. I simply wanted to know whether he was authorized by you to take any part in the Council, as it is the Indians alone we are here to meet. He told me you wanted him here as a witness."[17]

The negotiations ended with the following pledge being made by Morris, "We will send a copy [of the treaty] to each Chief. As to the Half-breeds you need not be afraid; the Queen will deal justly, fairly and generously with all her children."[18]

At the Treaties at Forts Carlton and Pitt, the same subject was broached by the Indians, who clearly felt that the discrimination against half-breeds by Morris was evident and harmful and had to be mitigated. So we read the following final exchange in the treaty negotiations.

"MIS-TOW-ASIS — "I wish to speak a word for some Half-breeds who wish to live on the reserves with us, they are as poor as we are and need help.

"GOVERNOR — How many are there?

"MIS-TOW-ASIS — "About twenty.

"GOVERNOR — ". . . We did not come as messengers to the Half-breeds, but to the Indians. I have heard some Half-breeds want to take lands and Red River and join the Indians there, but they cannot take with both hands. The Half-breeds of the North West cannot come into the Treaty. . . ."[19]

In the last chapter of his book Morris deals with the administration of the Treaties and the mechanism by which they were to be administered. He does not mention the Indian Act, the legal instrument which had already (despite its ad hoc beginnings) the force of scripture.

Chapter 8

Indian Acts to the Turn of the Century

British Columbia had been admitted into the Dominion in 1871 and the 1874 Indian legislation entitled "An Act to Amend certain laws relating to matters connected with Indians in the Provinces of Manitoba and British Columbia" brought these provinces under the existing Indian legislation.

The 1874 Act was short and almost entirely taken up with penalties for Indians caught intoxicated or for supplying liquor to Indians and included up to a month's imprisonment for an Indian convicted of being found in a state of intoxication.[1]

The first Act to bear the title of "Indan Act" was passed in 1876, consolidating and enlarging on previous legislation for Indians in one hundred sections.[2]

The definition of the term 'Indian' of 1868 was altered and elaborated upon by emphasizing descent in the male line and the importance of legitimacy.

"3. The term "Indian" means

First. Any male person of Indian blood reputed to belong to a particular band. [Changed from "All persons of Indian blood . . ."]
Secondly. Any child of such a person; [changed from "All persons residing among such Indians . . . descended on either side from Indians . . ."]
Thirdly. Any woman who is or was lawfully married to such a person

a) Provided that any illegitimate child, unless having shared with the consent of the band in the distribution moneys of such band for a period exceeding two years, may, at any time, be excluded from the membership thereof by the band, if such proceeding be sanctioned by the Superintendent-General.

b) Provided that any Indian having for five years continuously resided in a foreign country shall . . . cease to be a member thereof, etc."[3]

The Act goes on to re-state that a woman marrying a non-Indian "shall cease to be an Indian" but that she might retain her right to annuities. These however might "be commuted to her at any time at ten years' purchase with the consent of the band:" This was an amendment to the bill originally presented after one member of parliament had suggested in the House of Commons that it was "unwise" to penalize an Indian woman by depriving her of her rights and annuities "since such marriages were beneficial to the country."[4]

The insertion of the clause on the protest of illegitimate children appears to be (like the clause expelling from the band an Indian who was away for five years) as much an attempt to curb demands on the public purse as it was to impose Victorian moral standards, but whatever the reasons then the protesting of illegitimate children survives intact in 1978 and still keeps civil servants busy.[5]

On the "absence of five years" clause Sir John A. Macdonald said in Commons that he understood that it would be convenient for the Department to have this arrangement and that the Indians would approve of it, because the fewer there were in the band, the more its members would receive.[6]

The terms 'enfranchised' and 'non-treaty' Indian are also defined in this Act '. . . enfranchised Indian' means any Indian man, his wife and minor unmarried child, or an unmarried Indian woman over twenty-one years old "who has received letters granting him [or her] in fee simple any portion of the reserve which may have been allotted to him, his wife and minor children, by the band to which he belongs or any unmarried Indian who may have received letters patent for an allotment of the reserve".[7] Ownership of private property was clearly considered virtually synonymous with having achieved the stage of civilization known as enfranchisement.

It is important here to note that enfranchisement and loss of status through marriage were seen as being quite different since the woman who "married out" did not have to be specially prepared — educated or civilized — or prove she could survive in a white world but became the sole "burden and responsibility" of her husband.

'Non-treaty Indian' meant any person who hadn't taken treaty but was of "Indian blood, who is reputed to belong to an irregular band or who follows the Indian mode of life".

The possession of a location ticket was to be the only lawful way to hold a lot on a surveyed and subdivided reserve. On the holder's death one-third was to go to his widow and the rest to his children; if there were no children the wife inherited, and the property then passed to the band on her death. From the married woman's point of view this was an improvement on the Act of 1869.

This Act also provided that any Indian who became a professional — a lawyer, doctor, or minister of religion, or gained a university degree — was enfranchised ipso facto and was no longer an Indian. Finally a whole band could apply for enfranchisement. (The Caughnawaga Reserve applied but their request was denied.)[8]

The benefits for an Indian living on a reserve were spelled out: no taxation on real or personal property on a reserve; no liens on Indian property on a reserve, no annuities or property of an Indian might be

44

seized for debt, though Indians might sue for wrongs or non-performance of contract. In this Act an attempt was made to clarify the ambiguity concerning the entitlement to annuities of a woman marrying a non-Indian: "Provided that any Indian woman marrying any other than an Indian or a non-treaty Indian shall cease to be an Indian in any respect within the meaning of this Act except that she shall be entitled to share in the annual or semi-annual distribution of their annuities, interest monies and rents; but this income may be commuted to her at any time at ten years' purchase with the consent of the band."[9]

Whether accepting compensation was indeed an option open to such women obviously would depend however not on the wishes of the woman but the Band Council and Superintendent.

Section 72 of this Act also gave the Superintendent-General power "to stop the payment of the annuity and interest money of any woman having no children who deserts her husband and lives immorally with another man". Divorce through the courts was clearly even less accessible to an Indian woman than a white woman,[10] so this was an additional restriction on the Indian woman's autonomy.

The Indian Act of 1876 was soon found to be inadequate. Indeed the need to make almost annual amendments which arose after the Act of 1868 became an inescapable fact of subsequent Indian legislation. This, it has sometimes been suggested, is a tribute to the inherent flexibility and thus the fitness of the original Indian Act. Another interpretation might be that the fundamental premises in the Act concerning Indians ensured that there would be enormous problems in administering it and that constant changes would continue to be necessary until either the Act changed fundamentally or the Indians disappeared.

The Act of 1876 therefore needed amending in 1879.[11] Two new sections in this Act were concerned with Indian morality and related to Indian women and prostitution. In the Indian Act there is some ambiguity but the Criminal Code spells out clearly the penalties involved for both the Indian women and the owner of the dwelling — a fine of $10 to $100 or 6 months in jail. (Emphasis in the section is put on the words "unenfranchised Indian woman", and thus the fact that this only applied to women who were "wards".)[12]

The Indian Act was re-enacted in 1880 when a new and separate department for Indian Affairs under the Minister of the Interior was created because, Prime Minister Macdonald said, "The duties of the Indian Branch are so onerous".[13] So it is evident that there had been enormous changes in the thirty-six years since Oliphant's 1854 recommendation to reduce the scope of the Department.

Provisions are clearly spelled out in this 1880 Act for the removal as trespassers of any Indian and his family not of the band who "settles or hunts" on the band land.[14] There were few other changes in 1880 worthy of note except that an Indian woman who married into another band could continue to receive the annuities of her former band, though this might be commuted "at ten year's purchase". This provision remained until 1957 when commutation became mandatory and all ties with her former band were thus cut.[15]

In the East, Agent Cherrier reported from Caughnawaga in 1880 that the women worked day and night at poorly paid beadwork and stated, "it is a recognized principle amongst a great many Indians that it is the duty of the wife to support the husband."[16]

In the West, Indians were in a state of destitution because of disappearance of the buffalo and they were given rations by the Government. The 1880 Annual Report noted that "the system pursued in affording relief to the Indians is calculated to accustom them to habits of industry . . . under that system all able-bodied Indians are required to work for the food given themselves and their families."[17]

They had been expected to become farmers overnight, as had the Indians in the East, and were proving a sore disappointment to the Government.

The Deputy-Superintendent, Vankoughenet, wrote in 1880 in his instructions to an agent, "You should by every means in your power endeavour to persuade the Indians within your district to pursue industrial employment by cultivating the soil, etc. for a living; and no encouragement should be given by you to idleness by gratuitous aid being furnished to able bodied Indians."[18]

From 1878 to 1887 while Prime Minister John A. Macdonald was also Superintendent-General (Minister) of the Indian Department he left the administration mainly to the tender mercies of the Deputy-Superintendent, Lawrence Vankoughenet.[19]

Vankoughenet's recommendations for cutbacks in the Indian Department in 1884 in the West had disastrous results. Indians who were unable to adapt to the requirements of the new reserve life and the disappearance of the buffalo were starving but had their rations cut. Visits by agents to reserves were also cut to a minimum as an economy measure and enfranchisement was not reducing the number of Indians.[20]

It was noted in the Commons by one wag in 1879 that the policy of enfranchisement was proving such a success that he calculated that at the present rate of 54 Indians (including children) per twenty-two years it would take 36,000 years to enfranchise the Indian population of 90,000.[21]

The overriding concern for reducing the number of dependent Indians was shown when Sitting Bull and his men took refuge in Canada from certain death at the hands of the U.S. Government. The then Minister of the Interior in charge of Indian Affairs, David Mills wrote in 1877. ". . . It is not, however, desirable to encourage them to remain in Canada . . . it is desirable that as wards of the United States they should return to that country, upon the Government of which morally devolves the burden and responsibility of their civilization."[22] Sir John A. Macdonald, Minister of the Interior as well as Prime Minister, in 1878 complained that they were adding to the hardships endured by the Indians in the West by hastening the final disappearance of the buffalo on which the Plains Indians depended.[23]

The Métis Rebellion of 1885 was a symptom of the general mismanagement and neglect of native people in the West.[24]

The Indian Advancement Acts of 1884[25] and 1886[26] and the Franchise Act of 1885[27] endeavoured to accelerate the process of assimilation. The former gave some fiscal responsibility and other powers to band councils, the idea being that this would eventually lead to reserves becoming municipalities. However, the moral fitness of the Indians who served on the Band Council was to come under the scrutiny of the Superintendent, who could dismiss the chief and councillors if he so chose.

The Federal Franchise of 1885 extended the right to vote in federal elections to all men, including Indian men (but exempting Chinese and Indians in Manitoba, British Columbia, Keewatin and the Northwest Territories and any Indian without land worth $150). The extension of the franchise to Indians was withdrawn in 1896 after numerous protests that "wards", such as the Indians, were not legal persons (neither were women) and as such were not entitled to have such a responsibility.[28] No representation without taxation was the crux of the argument.

It is not known how many Indians were eligible to vote, but according to the Hawthorn-Tremblay report published in 1967, Indians in Ontario, Quebec and the Maritimes voted in general elections in 1887, 1891, and 1896.[29]

This report comments acidly, "The federal action in extending the franchise to Indians was not unalloyed generosity as the dependent position of the Indians was expected to lead to government support."[30] (Indians, male or female, were not accorded the right to vote in federal elections until 1960.)

Another facet of the civilizing and Christianizing process was an 1884 addition to the Indian Act forbidding Indians from holding traditional Indian festivals such as the Potlatch (and later the Sun Dance). Anyone who took part was subject to six months in jail.[31] These bans remained in effect until 1951.

Since these festivals, which symbolized and affirmed group unity, were integral to the culture and religious beliefs of the Indians on the West Coast and the Plains, such provisions had far-reaching cultural and psychological effects.

Another amendment of 1884 permitting Indians to make a will stressed again the same moral principles — a widow might inherit only if she was "a woman of good moral character".[32]

The Indian Act of 1886 was longer than ever, one hundred thirty-one sections, and is a consolidation of previous legislation. In Section 117 of this Act every Indian agent was granted to be "ex officio a justice of the peace for the purposes of this Act".[33] In 1887 a procedure for determining who was or was not entitled to be considered a member of a band was set up with a final route of appeal being extended from the Minister to the Governor in Council.[34]

Towards the turn of the century the aggressive policy of assimilation through the inculcation of the proper values in the semi-protected environment of the reserve began to give way to a growing impatience with Indians and the concomitant and convenient belief that reserves hindered "progress" — both of the Indian and the white settlers. Legislation began to reflect these beliefs.

The Superintendent-General in an amendment of 1894 was given wider discretionary powers than ever before, enabling him to take and lease reserve lands without band permission. School attendance became compulsory for Indian children up to the age of sixteen and, where there were no schools, they could be compelled to attend a residential school against the parents' wishes.[35] And this process of giving greater power to the Administration continued unabated. "The general intent of the almost yearly additions to the power of the Governor was to overcome the apparently increasing reluctance of band councils to do what the Department deemed desirable", comments a history commissioned by the Department of Indian Affairs.[36]

And the Department certainly did what it deemed desirable and the law was, it seems, altered to suit. The 1894 addition to the section on intoxicants in the 1888 amendment to the 1886 Indian Act created an additional definition of an Indian for the purpose of the liquor section of the Act. It reads thus: "6.2. In this section the expression 'Indian', in addition to its ordinary signification as defined in section two of this Act, shall extend to and include any person, male or female, who is reputed to belong to a particular band or who follows the Indian mode of life or any child of such person."[37] This section remained in force until 1951. Thus when it suited the Government a non-status woman and her children became Indians temporarily.

Again in the case of the Queen v. Howson of 1894 Judge J. Wetmore for a five man Court said, "I understand the popular and ordinary meaning of the words 'any male person of Indian blood', to mean any person with Indian blood in his veins, and whether such blood is obtained from the father or mother. I am not impressed with the view that Bear's mother being married to his father (a white man) ceased to be an Indian by virtue of section 11. Assuming that she did marry as alleged . . . while she herself lost her character of an Indian by such marriage, it did not affect her blood which she transmitted to her son."[38]

Indians, however, were not entitled to have any say in deciding who was or was not an Indian.

48

Chapter 9

Hardening Attitudes 1900-1945

The pressure by settlers on Indians to surrender their reserve lands in fertile areas was, after the turn of the century, clearly abetted by the government. Canadian Government Indian Rights Commissioner Stewart Raby, writing on land surrenders in Saskatchewan, notes: "A particularly conspicuous reflection of the Indians' failure to meet the expectations of the Department was the series of reserve land surrenders and subsequent sales which began in 1901 and gathered momentum in 1905"[1] (ending around 1928). However Raby points out that the Canadian government was "comparatively restrained" compared to the United States in this.[2]

The 1911 Act permitted the annexation by a town or city of reserve lands. "The Governor-in-Council may, upon the recommendation of the Superintendent-General, refer to the judge of the Exchequer Court of Canada for inquiry and report the question as to whether it is expedient, having regard to the interest of the public and of the interests of the band for whose use the reserve is held, that the Indians should be removed from the reserve or any part of it."[3]

Other measures continued to make alienation of reserve lands easier and there was an ever-increasing emphasis on status and enfranchisement. Amendments were clearly designed to cut down on the number of Indians and half-breeds who were allowed easier enfranchisement.

The Deputy Minister of Indian Affairs for the period from 1913-32 was Duncan Campbell Scott. His pessimistic hardline attitudes and the policy he established were the very quintessence of that self-righteous period. A memo by Scott to Indian Agents in 1913 illustrates this point. "It may be stated as a first principle that it is the policy of the Department to promote self-support among the Indians and not to provide gratuitous assistance to those Indians who can provide for themselves."[4] The agent, he pointed out, has "magisterial jurisdiction" and is an ex-officio justice of the peace. In this capacity he instructed the agent that "in some cases it might be advisable to inflict both fine and imprisonment" when a liquor law was contravened. As well, he said, "the Department has no objection to Agents or other outside officers of the Department acting as an informer in cases of prosecutions under the Indian Act nor to their receiving the moiety of the fine allowed the informer in certain cases." In other words, the Agent could be both judge and paid witness for the prosecution.[5]

The emergence of the policy of compulsory enfranchisement which ensued was a logical evolution of earlier initiatives and the failures of various experiments or attempts at gradually controlled assimilation. The management of Indian Affairs was transformed into the elimination of "the Indian Problem", as Scott called it, and this became an entrenched and basic assumption which he handed on to his successors. The Indian Act became like Scripture, a thing which had its own internal rationale, which could therefore not be breached, only added to.

On the question of who was an Indian, Scott had a standard speech with this answer: "Again Parliament has provided the legal definition of an Indian; descent in the male line alone gives the individual legal standing as an Indian. This definition has greatly simplified the Indian problem; true it has created a class of half-breeds dependent on the Provinces but it has enabled the Government to deal with its wards without complications." The solution to the Indian Problem, he ended, lies "in gradual assimilation with his fellow citizens."[6]

A 1918 amendment emphasized that any unmarried Indian woman or widow who met the necessary requirements might be enfranchised.[7] This was followed by the controversial enfranchisement amendments of 1920. In the East compulsory enfranchisement of the more "advanced" Indians who were determined to be self-supporting was to be accomplished through boards of inquiry. If the Indian so enfranchised held land on the reserve then the Superintendent General could grant him "letters patent" to the land. The difference between the value of the land and the share of the band funds was to be paid by the Indian. Any Indian, even if not a member of the band, who had been permitted to reside on the reserve could buy the reserve land on becoming enfranchised.[8]

When this 1920 legislation was being discussed in Commons Committee, D. C. Scott explained it thus: "Our object is to continue until there is not a single Indian in Canada that has not been absorbed into the body politic, and there is no Indian question and no Indian Department. That is the whole object of this Bill."[9]

George Manuel, the ex-president of the NIB, devotes several pages of his book "The Fourth World" to Scott's efforts to eradicate Indian customs such as the Potlatch despite the fact that he was a noted scholar who had published the first English-language version of the Iroquois Constitution.[10]

But there was considerable opposition from Indians to the implementation of this legislation and, since fostering opposition to enfranchisement was obviously counter-productive, the enfranchisement section was amended in 1922 to make applications by the Indian a prerequisite as before 1920.[11]

The woman who had lost her status through marriage was not of course affected by this since the procedure known as enfranchisement did not apply to her, but she and her children continued to be subject to involuntary loss of status with the addition in the 1920 Act that the Superintendent could unilaterally, without her or the band's permission, commute her annuities, so cutting off entirely her last connection with her band.[12]

This comment by a department official clearly states the rationale for this:

> "When an Indian woman marries outside the band whether a non-treaty Indian or a white man it is in the interests of the Department, and in her interests as well, to sever her connection wholly with the reserve and the Indian mode of life, and the purpose of this section was to enable us to commute her financial interests. The words 'with the consent of the band' have in many cases been effectual in preventing this severance as some bands are selfishly interested in preventing the expenditure of their funds. The refusal to consent is only actuated by stupidity because the funds are not really in any way impaired. The amendment makes in the same direction as the proposed Enfranchisement Clauses, that is it takes away the power from unprogressive bands of preventing their members from advancing to full citizenship.[13]

The 1927 consolidation of the Indian Act had little that is important here, but was a record 190 sections and 66 pages long.[14] This Act remained in effect with few changes until 1951.

It is interesting to note here that it was thought necessary to add to the earlier provision that a widow had to be of good moral character to inherit, another provision that "the Superintendent-General shall be the sole and final judge as to the moral character of the widow of any intestate Indian."[15]

There was also a rewording and tightening up of procedures regarding illegitimate children who might be protested at any time by the Superintendent-General if they had not received treaty monies for at least two years.[16]

In another section squatters on band allowances or other Indians not members of the band were to be evicted and jailed if they returned, even if only to fish.[17] This had serious implications for Indian women who had lost their status as well as for other Indians.

In passing it should be noted that an amendment of 1924 stipulated that the administration of Eskimo affairs would come under the aegis of the Superintendent-General of Indian Affairs but other provisions would not apply, to avoid bringing them, like the Indians, "into a state of tutelage and dependency."[18]

The period between the Act of 1927 and the end of the Second World War in 1945 saw no major policy changes or legislation. The Indian Affairs Department had been absorbed by the Department of Mines and Resources in 1936 and the focus was unequivocally on the development of mineral resources, not Indians. Indeed with the

Depression of the thirties and the War in the forties the "Indian problem" was pushed into complete obscurity. Conditions for half-breeds and non-status Indians in particular deteriorated considerably.[19]

Legislative amendments were mainly of the ad hoc variety, but these also tended to perpetuate the ethos of the 1920s, an overtly authoritarian approach which emphasized punishment for non-conformity.

A 1930s amendment, for example, states that an Indian who "misspends or wastes his time or means to the detriment of himself, his family or household" in a poolroom was to be banned from the poolroom for one year.[20]

Similarly, in 1933, the compulsory enfranchisement clause for all Indians of 1920, which had been dropped in 1922, was re-introduced. There was an increase in the power of the Superintendent-General, whose initiative alone was necessary to set up the Board of Inquiry and to institute proceedings in thirty days if the band council had not elected a representative of the band to the three man board.

In 1931 Scott wrote, "The department is confronted with serious problems in the slow process of weaning the Indian from his primitive state ... It may seem arbitrary on our part to interfere with the native culture. The position of our department, however, can be readily understood, and it is pointed out that Indians will spend a fortnight preparing for a sun-dance, another fortnight engaging in it, and another fortnight to get over it. Obviously this plays havoc with summer ploughing."[21]

Father René Fumoleau describes the period between 1922 and 1939 for Indians as "a period replete with discontent, broken promises, evasions and deceptions" and quotes Prime Minister St. Laurent: "Apparently we have administered the vast Territories of the North in a continuous state of absence of mind."[22]

Back on the reserves the government agents attempted to administer the 190 section Act and its various amendments to the best of their comprehension and abilities. Anomalies and inconsistencies in application were inevitable. Advice was frequently sought from Ottawa but there was evidently a great gulf between the officials in Ottawa and the officials in the field. Who was entitled to live on a reserve and receive government aid was a continual source of concern to agents.[23]

The problem was that women who had lost their status through marriage and were still receiving annuities continued to live on the reserve or on its fringes with native husbands who were half-breeds or non-status Indians. The agents in the field were the ones who had to contend with the unpleasant reality of enforcing evictions against the wishes of the band. Some agents however were not unduly upset by this task. After all they were merely fulfilling the law. A letter to Ottawa in 1937 from an Alberta reserve illustrates this quite well:

> "The half-breed population on these reserves seems to be quite a problem and I would like to get these off before winter sets in, but without police assistance this will be impossible. Will you please let me know your views to this before I start cleaning up on these people?"

> "Another aspect of the half-breed situation I would like your advice on, is the number of women of this agency who have married non-treaty Indians and are living on these reserves and when winter arrives they will be without means of support. The women are still paid treaty but according to 'Indian Act' are no longer members of the band. Some of these families have been living here for some years and some just drift here for the winter. What would you suggest doing with these people?"[24]

The reply from Ottawa is somewhat more concise though equally callous in tone and menacing in intent:

"... Re. half-breed population ... you should get in touch with the Superintendent of the R.C.M.P. at Edmonton who will give you all the assistance you require."[25]

The lack of cooperation from the band in evictions was evident in 1949 — a letter from the Indian Agent to the Department "Re. outsiders on Indian Reserves", concerning the Swan Lake band, notes: "The Treaty Indians never complain and as these outsiders are intermarried with the Swan Lake Indians I doubt if we could get a majority vote of the Band to remove them."[26]

Economizing on welfare and medical expenses was as much of a continuing concern as cutting down on the number of Indians on the reserve.

The clause in the Act which allowed an Indian woman's illegitimate child to be protested was also executed diligently and a form existed, which the Agent filled in for the mother sometimes immediately after the birth of an illegitimate child while she was still in hospital, in which she was required to give information as to the paternity of the child. The father, if an Indian from another band or a white man, was then traced and asked to sign a form affirming paternity of the child.[27]

A great deal of Department time and effort would seem to have been expended in this endeavour. One file includes details of the tracking down of a white man (whose nickname only was known) right across Canada, the hotly pursued trail ending abruptly when the man denied ever having heard of the Indian woman in question.[28]

Chapter 10

Pangs of Conscience — The Forties

In the wake of the Second World War a wave of humanism washed briefly over North America. This humanism and a revulsion from the recent revelations of man's inhumanity to man were articulated in the preamble to the 1948 United Nations Declaration of Human Rights: "Whereas disregard and contempt for human rights have resulted in barbarous acts which have outraged the conscience of mankind and the advent of a world in which human beings shall enjoy freedom of speech and belief and freedom from fear and want has been proclaimed as the highest aspiration of the common people".[1]

In Canada the condition of Indians was causing some concern and in 1946 a special Joint Committee of the Senate and the House of Commons which sat till 1948 was set up with broad terms of reference: to look at Indian Affairs and the Indian Act with a view to its amendment.[2]

On the practical side, the new Family Allowance Act of 1944 and welfare legislation increased the need for more complete and careful lists of the Indians who were eligible for benefits.

The Joint Committee had not contemplated accepting representations from Indians. But they soon found themselves under pressure to engage an Indian lawyer to act as intermediary for the Indians from the Six Nations.[3]

Of the 33 M.P.s and Senators on this committee, only one was a woman, Iva Fallis. The Chairman's first remark at the very beginning of the proceedings is rather interesting and addressed to her: "I think we shall have it understood that whenever the masculine term is used it will indicate both masculine and feminine. I hope our lady member will agree to that."[4] It seems rather curious that he should have felt such a remark was even necessary. But whether or not the confusion inherent in the Indian Act as well as in its interpretation which arose as a result of this English semantic convention had been a topic of dissent is not known. This decision however was not in the interests of clarity or precision since a separate legal regime did exist for Indian women from Indian men — not only with respect to marriage and illegitimate children, but on, for example, exclusion from right to vote in band elections and so partake in band business, rights to inherit and for a widow to administer her husband's estate.

Many of the legal disabilities for women existed as much by omission as by explicit statement in the Act, though, as has been noted throughout this paper, the latter were not lacking. The consequences of this insistence on the use of only the masculine term were unfortunate; as in the past it had led to confusion in the interpretation of the Act so also it did in the 1951 Act, which followed on the recommendations of this Joint Committee. Indeed, there is still today a strongly held belief on some reserves that women are not entitled to hold a certificate of possession, formerly called a location ticket, to land on a reserve.[5]

It is also important to note that in common law the word "man" or words of the masculine gender did not include women, as was established by a court case just after the failure of an attempt by the reformer J. S. Mill to have the word "person" substituted for the word "man" in the 1867 Reform Act.[6]

After the Joint Committee it was Senator Iva Fallis who at the very beginning of the proceedings brought up the question of Indian women losing their status through marrying non-Indians.

Her questions were put during the evidence of the first witness, Robert Hoey, Director of Indian Affairs. Hoey began by asking a crucial question: "Is it possible that in the past we have given too much thought to what might be termed the machinery of administration and not enough thought perhaps to the task for which this administrative machinery was created?"

Hoey, it is evident from his statements, subscribed to the assimilation ethic, but emphasized the merits of gentle persuasion rather than force and also the "rights" of the Indian not as applying to property rights alone, but "as a human being living in a free country".

However he criticized the definition of "Indian", which he thought was being used "somewhat loosely".

From Hoey's evidence it would seem that he saw the Indian Act as an Act which deprived people of their human rights. Nevertheless he believed that, given the existence of such discrimination, discrimination should be based on blood quantum, since, as he pointed out, an Indian could have a white mother and a white grandmother, and still be legally an Indian. This question had "disturbed" him, he said, "since entering the Department". He questioned "the moral authority of parliament . . . to deprive persons with 50 per cent or more white blood of the full rights of Canadian citizenship". He believed that a fair definition would be "An Indian is a person with 50 per cent or more native or Indian blood". It is evident that he believed that given the choice no-one would want to remain an Indian who could become a Canadian citizen.

On an Indian woman losing her status through marrying out, Hoey stated that a problem occurred when she returned to the reserve "having been deserted by her husband or immediately following her husband's death. She is no longer an Indian in a statutory sense nor is she the responsibility of the Indian Affairs Branch. Indeed it can be said that the money voted for by Parliament is voted on the distinct understanding that it is for the welfare of Indians and cannot be spent for the relief of white citizens". Hoey evidently was inconsistent in his application of "blood" since he here makes an Indian woman white, or perhaps he thought that only in the male was the genetic composition important.

In the same vein, a short time later when revisions to the Act were being discussed in 1955, it was seriously considered whether there might not be special provisions made giving Indian status to the illegitimate male child but not female child of an Indian man and white woman.[7] This incomparable blend of racism and sexism was both a function and a product of the Indian Act.

Iva Fallis put the question about Indian women after Hoey's statements on "white" Indian women: "Am I correct in understanding from what you said a moment ago that if an Indian woman marries a white man she ceases to be an Indian yet she is not a white woman? If her husband deserts her, or dies, she is left destitute and there is no-one to look after her? That does not apply in the case where an Indian marries a white woman. It seems unjust to the Indian woman who marries a white man because neither the white people nor the Indians want her." The Chairman interrupted to say that this would be considered by the committee. Hoey said, "It is an awkward problem" and went on to other matters. The question of membership was postponed till 1947 and then to 1948. Hoey's remarks, or at least the notions on which they are premised, were incorporated in the 1951 Act, which is still in force today, in the changed wording of the definition of an Indian.

A number of representatives from bands and associations submitted briefs and gave testimony to the Joint Committee in 1946 and 1947. Most of these groups emphasized that decisions as to membership of the band should be the decision of the band and that involuntary enfranchisement should be abolished. The North American Indian Brotherhood, the Indian Association of Alberta, the Native Brotherhood of British Columbia, and the Union of Saskatchewan Indians all made strong statements on this. This was considered a major breakthrough. Indians after all had not been consulted before as to their wishes.

Some groups, the Caughnawaga Indians and the St. Regis Indians for example, called for the complete abolition of the Act.[8]

The Native Brotherhood of B.C. stated that women who had lost their status through marriage and who were deserted or widowed should be allowed to rejoin their band with their children.[9]

But very different sentiments were being expressed by the Indian Affairs Department in this memo prepared for the Committee: "It might be contended that by the alteration of the definition of Indian by the Statute of 1876 the Dominion very substantially reduced the number of people for whose welfare it was responsible and by that action passed the responsibility on to the provinces for thousands of people, who, but for the statute of 1876, would have been a federal responsibility for all time."[10]

T. L. R. MacInnes, the Secretary of Indian Affairs, in similar vein, in a series of talks entitled "Canada's Indian Problem" worried about the cost of services to Indians and asked, "When will they [the Indians] be able to stand on their own feet? In my opinion not for a long time . . . Indeed if we are to make these people self-supporting at all, it is clear to me that we must increase rather than relax our supervision."[11]

This echoes almost exactly the recommendation of the Committee of 1844-45: "their further progress requires more enlarged measures, and more active interference."[12]

The one hundred years later Committee of 1946-48 in its final report found that the Indian Act was replete with "anachronisms, anomalies, contradictions and divergencies", and recommended "that, with few exceptions, all sections of the Act be either repealed or amended".[13]

The first recommendations were concerned with treaty rights and recognized the need for a thorough investigation of Indians' claims through a Claims Commission, the right to vote at Federal elections, improved integrated educational facilities, old age pensions, advisory boards, better cooperation with provinces where overlapping jurisdiction was a problem, and the handling of related affairs all by one Ministry.[14]

The recommendation on band membership, however, is not so enlightened in tone, and the Indians' recommendations were ignored. It reads:

> "To replace the definition of Indian which has been statutory since 1876, there must be a new definition more in accord with present conditions. Parliament annually votes moneys to promote the welfare of Indians. This money should not be spent for the benefit of persons who are not legally members of an Indian Band. Your Committee believes that a new definition of 'Indian' and amendment of those sections of the Act which deal with band membership will obviate many problems.[15]

> "Your Committee recommends that in the meantime the Indian Affairs Branch should undertake the revision of existing Band membership lists."

They also recommended a clarification in the "rules and regulations" of both voluntary and involuntary enfranchisement. Outside of their terms of reference they also recommended that Indian women over 21 be given the right to vote in band elections which men had had since 1869 and that the offence and penalties sections of the Act (concerning liquor among other things) be brought into conformity with the penalties imposed on other Canadians in the Criminal Code.[16]

Chapter 11

The Indian Act of 1951

It might be expected, given the interest in human rights and the lengthy deliberations of the Joint Committee, that some major changes would ensue in this the first revision of the Indian Act since 1927 but when Bill 267 was presented for first reading in the House there was a storm of protest. It was characterized as a "shamefully inadequate piece of legislation", "inept" and "a vast disappointment to friends of Indians".[1] M. P. John Diefenbaker saw it as a licence to give even more power to administrative officials than ever before, putting "shackles" on approximately 125,000 Indian people, making of the Indian "a second-class citizen under the law". "For three years", he said, "that committee sat. Now the mountain brings forth a mouse".[2]

There were some hurried three-day consultations with Indians. A Special Committee was set up and a new bill was produced. The content remained the same however, though there were some changes in wording and the Special Committee recommended that "further consideration be given to the Indian Act in two years". This Bill 79 was passed on 17 May 1951. With some amendments, this mighty "mouse" is the Act in force today, twenty-seven years later.[3]

The discretionary powers of the Minister or Governor-in-Council were once more amplified. On the other hand the more blatant discrepancies between the Criminal Code and the Indian Act were removed. There was an easing of laws on intoxicants, the prohibition on Indian ceremonies and dances was removed, the requirements of obtaining permission from the agent to travel or sell produce were also omitted. Indian women were for the first time given the right to vote in band elections.

The enfranchisement section and the membership section were greatly elaborated upon and altered. Both increased the disadvantages for Indian women who "married out". The sections dealing with estates and inheritance were also amended and adversely affect the same women.[4]

The consequences for Indian women and their children of these sections regarding membership, enfranchisement and inheritance are far-reaching, and they are completely interwoven with the effects on other Indians that such an invitation to injustice and discrimination constitutes. The results thus affect the whole development of human relationships in Indian communities.

The membership section, in becoming vastly more elaborate, spelled out at length not only who was entitled to be registered as an Indian but also who was not. The mention of "Indian blood" was removed and the male line of descent was further emphasized as the major criterion for inclusion. The first part of this section (section 11) has already been cited here (in Chapter 2).

Further changes in section 12 which decreed who was not entitled to be inscribed in the band lists have their own strange logic and are written in the bureaucratic vernacular. This, together with Hoey's concern with "blood", is evident in the formulation of the "double mother" rule which stipulates that among those not entitled to be registered is "a person who . . . is a person born of a marriage entered into after the coming into force of this Act and has attained the age of twenty-one years, whose mother and whose father's mother are not persons described in paragraph (a), (b), or (d) or entitled to be registered by virtue of paragraph (e) of section eleven unless, being a woman, that person is the wife or widow of a person described in section 11, and (b) a woman who married a person who is not an Indian", "unless, [a 1956 amendment added] that woman is subsequently the wife or widow of a person described in section 11".

What this means is that a child of a white or non-registered Indian mother and grandmother, who therefore has only one-quarter Indian Act "blood", is to be deprived of Indian status on reaching the age of 21. This section would apply to children whose maternal grandmothers were voluntarily or involuntarily enfranchised Indians, or Indians who were left off band lists or lived in the U.S. for over five years, or Métis who might have three Indian grandparents, as much as the children of white women. This has in fact clearly nothing to do with biology or Indian "blood" but everything to do with the Indian Act.

Though this part of the legislation has never been enforced,[5] another opportunity for divisiveness exists. It also serves to draw attention to the awesome confusion in the minds of legislators and the failure or unwillingness to accept the reality that the definition of "Indian" in the Act was primarily a creation of the Act itself, and that Victorian notions based implicitly on male "blood" as the criterion for membership were biologically unsound and historically inaccurate. Justice Bora Laskin found it necessary to emphasize this point in his dissenting opinion in the Lavell case some twenty-two years later.[6]

In a similar vein are sections concerning descendants of those who had been allotted half-breed lands or scrip, who were not to be entitled to be registered. The result of this enactment was that attempts were made by the Department to deprive whole clans of their Indian status on the basis that their forebears had taken half-breed scrip. This was so disastrous that public opinion forced it to a halt and this was amended in 1958 allowing those at that date registered as Indians to remain so.[7]

The major change for an Indian woman who "married out" was that until this time she had to some extent had a dual status as an Indian and an ordinary Canadian citizen. Until 1951 she had usually retained the right to go on collecting annuities and band monies if she did not choose to accept a lump sum "commutation", and thus continue to be on the band list. As a result she continued to enjoy some band benefits as well as treaty rights (if her band had taken treaty), though she was no longer an "Indian Act" Indian.

Some Indian agencies had issued prior to 1951 an identity card called a "Red Ticket" to such women which identified them as Indians for the purposes of sharing in treaty and band monies.[8] Neither they nor any other Indian women were entitled to vote in band elections prior to 1951. The major disabilities therefore on loss of status prior to 1951 for Indian women who married non-Indians were that they were deprived of their legal rights to hold land on the reserve and that their children would not have Indian status. As if this were not grim enough, they were now to be subject to involuntary enfranchisement.

Involuntary enfranchisement for men, introduced first in 1920, withdrawn and then re-introduced in the 1933 legislation, was omitted from this Act of 1951 though voluntary enfranchisement for men and bands was retained.

But new clauses were now inserted in the enfranchisement section of the Act affecting Indian women who married non-Indians though the provisos that the Indian who chose to enfranchise be "capable of supporting himself and his dependents" and "capable of assuming the duties and responsibilities of citizenship" as well as the necessity of obtaining the consent of the band are conveniently set aside in the woman's case.[9] Enfranchisement for women who lose their status thus differs substantially from voluntary enfranchisement.

The Indian woman who married a non-Indian now was automatically deprived of her Indian status and her band rights from the date of her marriage. "On the report of the Minister that an Indian woman married a person who is not an Indian, the Governor-in-Council may by order declare that the woman is enfranchised as of the date of her marriage."[10] Her prior children were not mentioned in this 1951 Act but they were erroneously enfranchised with her until 1956, when the section was amended to read "and on the recommendation of the Minister [the Governor-in-Council] may by order declare that all or any of her children are enfranchised as of the date of the marriage or such other date as the order may specify".[11] A Parliamentary Committee considering the revision to the Act in 1955 had noted that the enfranchisement section would have to be altered to include children, i.e. bring the law into line with practice "By taking no action the Governor in Council might permit some children to remain Indian forever. It is doubtful whether this was the intention".[12] In 1967, after many complaints had been laid, those children who were erroneously enfranchised with their mothers between 1951 and 1956 were re-instated when they could be traced.[13]

It was the same committee which pondered whether the illegitimate male child of an Indian and non-Indian should have status but reached no decision. They also started off their discussions by resolving "to preserve what was done in the past".[14]

The effect of this 1956 amendment was that Indian children who lived with their mother and their non-Indian step-father after her marriage off a reserve were also enfranchised but the Minister, at his discretion, could permit those children who continued to live on the reserve to retain their status. (The Minister in the main relies on Department officials for the resolution of such matters, but what exactly the word "may" means in the legislation when referring to ministerial discretion is difficult to assess and does seem to have varied over time.)

Another amendment of 1956 to section 12 stated that the illegitimate child of a female Indian could be protested and excluded from the band within twelve months of the addition of its name to the Band List if "it is decided that the father of the child was not an Indian".[15]

What all these provisions meant in practice was that a large number of Indian children both of whose parents were Indian were also enfranchised after 1951, their sole transgression being that some of them were born illegitimate.

The many anomalies and injustices which were thus visited on the children further augmented the difficult lot of women who "married out".

The other important effects of a woman's loss of status are on the Indian woman's ability to own or inherit property on the reserve.

Many women who married before the 1951 Act chose not to accept commutation and to retain their "Red Ticket" status. This administrative inconsistency was changed by an amendment of 1956 to section 15 of the Act. "Red Ticket" women were paid a lump sum of ten times the average annual amount of all payments which they had been paid over the preceding ten years and so brought into line with the rest.[16]

All Indian women who "married out" after this date became subject to the enfranchisement procedure which occurs after an Order-in-Council has been made. This is usually declared to take effect on the date of her marriage. She is then deemed according to section 110 "not to be an Indian within the meaning of this Act or any other statute or law". On the issuing of the order of enfranchisement any property which she holds on the reserve must be sold or otherwise disposed of in thirty days. In exchange she is given twenty years of treaty money (if the band took treaty) plus "one per capita share of the capital and revenue moneys held by Her Majesty on behalf of the band".[17]

Since she is not entitled to live on a reserve and any property she inherits there is subject to be sold by the Superintendent to the highest bidder, the issuing of the order of enfranchisement is the last step before property must be disposed of.

Enfranchisement is a term which has always had a very different meaning for Indians from whites. Even the meaning given gy government has also varied somewhat over time. In general however the same ethos underlay enactments on enfranchisement — that assimilation to Euro-Canadian culture should be the ultimate goal for Indians. This goal was perceived as a privilege only to be conferred by the superior society on the Indians when they had achieved certain standards of civilized behaviour. Maintaining the Indian in a state of "wardship" without legal rights until he or she had "progressed" sufficiently to be made a full citizen (i.e., enfranchised) was considered an onerous though necessary duty.

However, most Indians unobligingly perceived enfranchisement as something to be avoided. They preferred to retain their Indian identity, culture and values despite all inducements, and, apart from the compulsory enfranchisement of professionals, very few Indians chose to become enfranchised in the nineteenth century.

The same situation persisted into the twentieth century, although the existence of compulsory enfranchisements between 1920-24 and 1933-1951 (i.e., before women "marrying out" were subject to enfranchisement) makes it rather difficult to assess this statistically. Since 1951 very few Indians have chosen to become enfranchised. Should they wish to do so, however, they are still obliged to prove their worthiness and ability to survive outside the reserve; i.e., that they no longer need to be "protected".

Indian women, on the other hand, who lose their status through marriage are not required to demonstrate that they can be self-supporting in order to be enfranchised and enfranchisement is irreversible (except if the woman is widowed or divorced and then remarries a registered Indian).

Many members of the public feel that the word "enfranchisement" today must connote some benefit for Indian women. Nevertheless they suffer as Indians because they lack educational opportunities and have to face job and other forms of discrimination to which all Indians off the reserve are subject.[18] In fact the whole idea of enfranchisement was a patent anachronism by 1951, but the term is now perpetuated as a polite fiction which disguises the blatant discrimination towards Indian women in the Act. Prior to 1951 there was no pretence that such women were "enfranchised". Department of Indian Affairs officials also seem to cherish the ability to claim that "enfranchisement refers to men too". Statistics show otherwise.[19]

If we examine Table II below we see that 5,035 women and children were subject to enfranchisement between 1965 and 1975 following on the application of section 12(1)(b). This compares with a total of 228 voluntary enfranchisements of both men and women.

That is, only 5% of enfranchisements are voluntary and 95% of enfranchisements have been of women who had no choice.

From 1973 to 1976 however the difference is even greater. There have been only 11 voluntary adult enfranchisements (3 in 1976) and 1,335 involuntary adult enfranchisements plus, in 1976, 273 women who were not enfranchised but lost their status, totalling 1,608 for 1973 to 1976.[20] The percentage of voluntary enfranchisements of women and men for these years is 0.68%. Or, to put it another way, enforced enfranchisement of women accounted for 99.32% of all enfranchisements between 1973 and 1976. Moreover, the figure for voluntary enfranchisement appears to be diminishing, going from 7 persons in 1972-73 to 3 in 1975-76.

Out of a total Indian population of some 280,000 then, four people in the past two years have chosen enfranchisement. These figures are, I believe, sufficient comment on the merits of enfranchisement as they are perceived by Indians. (See Tables I, II and III.)

TABLE I
Enfranchisements — 1955-65

Period	Adult Indians enfranchised upon application together with their minor unmarried children		Indian women enfranchised following marriage to non-Indians together with their minor unmarried children		Total number of Indians enfranchised
	Adults	Children	Women	Children	
1955-56	192	130	337	97	756
1956-57	192	145	389	113	839
1957-58	169	149	305	50	673
1958-59	138	52	612	—	802
1959-60	221	248	433	221	1123
1960-61	125	70	592	167	954
1961-62	94	47	435	140	716
1962-63	90	50	404	109	653
1963-64	40	38	287	102	473
1964-65	46	34	480	176	736
TOTAL	1313	963	4274	1175	7725

TABLE II
Enfranchisements — 1965-75

Period	Adults	Children	Women	Children	Total
1965-66	38	18	435	147	638
1966-67	31	22	457	148	658
1967-68	62	28	470	56	616
1968-69	37	20	531	197	785
1969-70	41	19	547	107	714
1970-71	25	12	517	98	652
1971-72	14	4	281	19	304
1972-73	7	—	—*	—	7
1973-74	7	4	449	—	460
1974-75	1	—	590	—	591
TOTAL	263	127	4263	772	5425

Note: Since 1974, the enfranchisement of children has ceased.

*Enfranchisements were suspended in 1972-73 while the Lavell case was before the courts.

TABLE III
Accumulated Enfranchisements

1876 to 1918	102
1918 to 1948	4,000
Fiscal 1948 to 1968	13,670
Fiscal 1968 to 1969	785
Fiscal 1969 to 1970	714
Fiscal 1970 to 1971	652
Fiscal 1971 to 1972	304
Fiscal 1972 to 1973	7
Fiscal 1973 to 1974	460
TOTAL	20,694

All statistics obtained from D.I.A.N.D.

Since 1975, however, there have been no Orders-in-Council forcing women to enfranchise. (Remember that loss of status, which involves being struck off the register, and enfranchisement are separate procedures.) The reasons for this are unclear, but there would appear to be a developing distaste for the issuance of Orders-in-Council relating to Indians.[21] It would appear therefore that section 110, which states that "a person with respect to whom an order for enfranchisement is made . . . shall . . . be deemed not to be an Indian", and section 111 requiring the selling of property on a reserve by those who are "enfranchised" can no longer legally be enforced. Yet Indian women who marry non-Indians are still being struck off band lists and being "paid off" for their loss of Indian status.

Interestingly, the number of marriages of Indian men to non-Indian women seems to be increasing and for the years 1973 to 1976 inclusive has exceeded the number of women marrying non-Indians by 9.7%. (See graph and Table IV.)

The conclusion to be drawn from all this is once more that there is one law for men and another for women and that men do not hesitate to take advantage of the double standard. Should Indian women however believe, as some do, that it is possible to conceal the fact of their marriage to a non-Indian through marriage in the city, they are not likely to be successful since the Department of Indian Affairs apparently has an arrangement with Statistics Canada and most if not all marriages of Indians are eventually reported.[22]

TABLE IV

	Indian women who married non-Indians		Indian men who married non-Indians
1965	450	1965	258
1966	523	1966	273
1967	524	1967	300
1968	520	1968	341
1969	580	1969	388
1970	597	1970	414
1971	306	1971	231
1972	440	1972	442
1973	538	1973	564
1974	585	1974	544
1975	323	1975	362
1976	451	1976	611

Statistics obtained from D.I.A.N.D.

INDIAN MARRIAGES TO NON-INDIANS

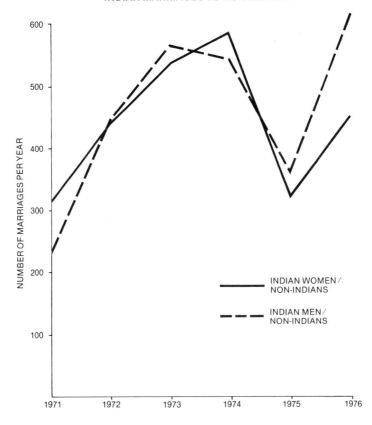

66

Chapter 12

The Consequences of Loss of Status

Compensation

One of the arguments that Indian women who have lost their status most frequently encounter is that they have been financially recompensed for whatever they have lost.

No sum of money can ever compensate for their loss and that of their children of their culture and identity. But the fact is that in all areas save Alberta the amount they are paid on enfranchisement as their share of band funds is often negligible or nothing at all.

According to section 15 of the Indian Act, an Indian woman who is enfranchised or "otherwise ceases to be a member of a band" is entitled to receive one per capita share of band capital and revenue. If the band to which the woman belonged had also taken treaty, she is paid a sum equivalent to twenty years' treaty money — a total of between $80 (20 x $4) and $100 (20 x $5).[1]

The total amount paid out to both women and men (4,470 women through marriage — i.e. involuntary enfranchisement — and 225 women and men through voluntary enfranchisement, according to calculations which are based on D.I.A.N.D. figures), between 1966 and 1977 was $1,229,117.37. This is an average of $261.80 per person. However, averages are rather meaningless here.[2]

An Indian woman who marries an Indian from another band and thus, according to the Indian Act, becomes a member of her husband's band, is paid the difference between the per capita share of her former band and that of her new band if the share of her former band is greater.

Many of these Indian women who change bands and those who lose their status through marriage believe that even the scanty compensation allotted to them on marrying either a non-Indian or an Indian from another band is rendered still smaller than it should be by accounting procedures which do not include all band assets and investments when their share is being computed. In addition, in Alberta they believe that they are entitled to compensation for loss of royalties from the present exploitation of natural resources — gas or oil, for example — as well as for the loss of the right to share in profits from future royalties gained from gas, oil, coal, timber, etc.[3]

These women have no way of ascertaining whether or not their suspicions that they are not being fairly treated in this are justified, since they are not permitted access to the band accounts nor are they allowed to receive any information whatsoever from the section of the Department of Indian Affairs in Ottawa which has these figures. Neither does there appear to be any appeal or investigative procedure to which the women may have recourse on this matter.

The share of band funds to which they are entitled is supposedly calculated by dividing the total band assets by the number of persons in the band. But capital investment by the band in business ventures such as a hotel, lodge or factory, or in some other assets such as farm machinery, buildings or animals on a ranch, for example, is not included. In practice then, only what is actually shown in the band's bank balance on the day the woman is enfranchised is used as the basis for the calculation of her share.[4]

The consequence of this is that even a woman from a very rich band where oil royalties may average millions of dollars per year receives a relatively small sum.[5]

Many women get nothing or only the annuity payment, which is a maximum of $100. Such is the case with many of the bands in the Mackenzie district, such as the Arctic Red River Band, which pays only an annuity of $100 and no band share. The Attawapiskat in May 1975 managed to pay out 7¢ and the annuity of $80. The Fitz Smith Band paid 1¢. Fort Franklin and the Dog Rib Rae paid nothing. In Prince Edward Island the Abegweit in December 1975 paid $4.06. In Nova Scotia in February 1967 the Eskasoni Band paid $22.40. In Quebec the Montagnais of Escoumains paid $4.45 in 1965 and in Ontario the Albany Band paid 32¢ as the per capita share.

In the middle range the Shammon Band in B.C. paid $985.95 in 1974 and $251.08 in 1976. The Spallumcheen in B.C. paid $102.12 in May 1975 and $425.22 in February 1976.[6]

These are indeed not munificent sums. One might expect a difference in Alberta, where some bands get millions of dollars in oil and gas revenues. But relative to the amount of royalties the bands may expect to have, the compensation women are paid is not excessive, though it seems large in comparison with the very small sums that women in other provinces receive. The top amount paid out in Alberta was $12,297.48 on March 1, 1976. In April, June and August of 1976 the Sampson Band paid out an average of about $12,000. The Louis Bull Band in June 1975 paid $9,190.98, but ten years before paid only $1,113.50 and in 1955 paid $419.89. The Sampson Band in 1956 paid $1,000.22. Both these bands are on the Hobbema Reserve.

Clearly the women and their children from these bands who were enfranchised ten or twenty years ago have lost a great deal in terms of potential income for which they have not been compensated. The same may be said to be true of those who are being "paid off" today in 1978.

If we assume that, as in any other transaction in which a person is selling his or her share of an estate or business, all assets should be included, then the Indian women are being very inadequately compensated. If, in addition, unexploited rich natural resources are considered a part of these assets, compensation would also be computed based on the potential revenue which would accrue from the exploitation of these resources.

This kind of calculation is made quite frequently by energy economists such as Pedro Van Meurs, who specializes in oil and gas supply and demand evaluation and analyses.

Van Meurs has explained for the purpose of this study how a formula for compensating for loss of oil royalties might be calculated, using as a reference R. G. McCrossan's "The Future Petroleum Provinces of Canada".[7] In reserves, for example, in that region of Alberta called the Craton Margin, which stretches from Peace River to the Saskatchewan border and which in the central area covers the whole province, potential oil and gas is estimated at 121,000 barrels and 580 million cubic feet per square mile. Two-thirds of these are proven. A band should, at a conservative estimate, obtain about one-third of the gross revenue from the oil and gas in royalties, as does the Province of Alberta. A rough calculation of the oil and gas royalties based on an area roughly the size of the Hobbema Reserve near Edmonton (160 square miles) gives an average potential 19.3 million barrels of oil and 92 billion cubic feet of gas. Royalties (a possible one-third of gross value) are estimated therefore at $10 per barrel of oil and $1 per 1,000 cubic feet of gas. To estimate the share of each person, the total sum expected in royalties is then divided by the number of persons on the reserve. In this case, Van Meurs assumed a band size of 3,000. Each person might therefore expect $31,000. Converting this into a once-and-for-all cash payment at 11% discount rate in current dollars and including 6% inflation gives $15,000 per person.

Given a higher rate of inflation than 6%, this sum could be substantially higher. (See Appendix for method of calculation.)

This is only one area in which compensation is clearly inadequate. Alberta is also rich in coal and the same kind of calculations could be made based on potential royalties from this resource. Other provinces similarly could have their mineral and forest resource potential computed so that the women who are in effect forced to "sell out" are treated as fairly as possible in the circumstances.

Social and Cultural Losses

Apart from financial losses, one of the more important benefits which are lost to enfranchised women and their children is in the field of education. In recent years the bilingual and bicultural programmes available on reserves open the door to a heritage of Indian culture to which the child of an enfranchised Indian mother does not have access.[8] About 65% of Canada's native people over thirty speak a native language so at least half of the mothers of these children speak a native language and will not have this opportunity to have their children educated in their language or culture.[9]

Indian school children are also entitled to receive all school supplies, a noon lunch supplement, sports equipment, art supplies, shop supplies, money for tours and interschool activities, as well as the payment of expenses where attendance at a special school is necessary.

Free daycare facilities and nursery schools are provided on some reserves for pre-school children.[10]

In post-secondary education there is an even greater disparity in opportunity. A status Indian, his spouse and children are entitled to post-secondary educational allowances covering tuition, books, living expenses, travel and clothing.[11] The Indian woman who has lost her status does not have this opportunity to upgrade her education and so obtain reparation for past government deficiencies in this respect nor, of course, do her children.

In the provision of housing, Indians living off reserves can qualify for a repayable first mortgage from C.H.M.C. and a forgivable second mortgage from the Department of Indian Affairs.[12]

A new Indian reserve housing policy was announced on November 18, 1976. This policy included a "front-end" subsidy of up to $12,000 per unit based on income, and other special facilities enabling Indian families, particularly in low income groups, to purchase their own homes.[13]

This programme and some of the education and other programmes have evolved fairly recently as a result of government-Indian working committees set up after the joint NIB/Cabinet committee was established in 1975.[14]

An interesting aside to this, considering that special problems exist with regard to housing for female-headed single parent families,[15] is that these decisions on housing are not seen as requiring input from women's organizations. A recent Departmental paper makes it clear that housing has been viewed as a male concern. The paper is entitled "The Indian Housing Programme and the Role of the Indian Woman" and is designed to involve Indian women in the housing programme. It states: "As a member of an on-reserve Indian community, you can play a very constructive role in housing. You may wonder how! Normally we associate building houses as a role for men."[16]

Enfranchised Indian women who are widowed or divorced may not partake of these benefits. The white widow or divorced white spouse of a status Indian male can.[17]

Other benefits from which they are excluded include: loans and grants from the Indian Economic Development Fund to start a business; exemption from taxation while living on the reserve; exemption from provincial sales tax on goods delivered to a reserve in Quebec, Ontario, Saskatchewan, Nova Scotia, New Brunswick and Manitoba (Alberta has no sales tax); free medicines to which the members of some bands — for example the Treaty Six Bands of Saskatchewan and Alberta — are entitled; hunting, fishing, animal grazing and trapping rights on and (under certain conditions) off a reserve; cash distributions derived from the sale of band assets of monies surplus to band needs. Canadian Indians may also be employed in the U.S. without a visa and have certain border crossing privileges under the United States Immigration and Naturalization Act.[18]

Psychological Effects

There are losses, however, which can never be computed and which are a consequence of the social and cultural alienation which occurs as a result of enfranchisement. These losses have not been documented.

But life histories such as the biography of Verna Patronella Johnston, "I am Nokomis, too",[19] and the autobiography of Maria Campbell, "Half-breed",[20] though not directly related to women's loss of status, do provide a good deal of information on the psychological magnitude of the problem. The enfranchised Indian woman and her children find themselves with identity problems, culturally different and often socially rejected by white society, yet they may not participate with family and relatives in the life of their former communities.

The threat and harassment associated with eviction from the reserve have caused at least one heart attack and sudden death and severe psychological and health problems in women and children.[21] The long term effects on the traditionally close Indian family on the reserve, the disruption and misery caused where sister may turn against sister and an invidious distinction is made between brother and sister, are profound and impossible to measure.[22]

The whole process of forcible enfranchisement is one of retribution, not restitution. The extent of the penalties and the lack of compensation for the losses suffered as a result of 12 (1) (b) make this quite evident. It is, in Justice Bora Laskin's words, "statutory banishment" which is compounded by the enfranchisement order, "an additional legal instrument of separation from her native society and from her kin, a separation to which no Indian man who marries a non-Indian is exposed."[23]

Inheritance of Property and Evictions

The question of inheritance of property and the right to live on the reserve is one that has provided more opportunities for victimization than most.[24]

The Department of Indian Affairs, following mainly on the legislation of 1869, has insisted for more than one hundred years that Indian women who married non-Indians should not be allowed to remain on or return to the reserve even when widowed or separated since they are now "white".

It is clearly advantageous to have as few band members to share in band monies and resources as possible, and a temptation to the needy as well as the unscrupulous. The eviction of widowed or separated women who return to the reserve often with several small children to live in a family home has thus become common practice on a few reserves. Since these women are usually very poor, obtaining legal advice is an enormous problem.[25] They are quite clearly in an extremely disadvantaged position.

Indeed, in attempting to use property bequeathed to her in a will, as for example in the case of Yvonne Bedard or in the recent case of Cecilia Pronovost, an Indian woman may find that she has taken on not only the Band Council but the whole Department of Indian Affairs and the Department of Justice as well, the latter Department having the responsibility of advising Indian Affairs on such matters.

The case of Cecilia Pronovost is not straightforward. Perhaps for that very reason however it is particularly illuminating to study the immense problem which is faced by an Indian woman who has lost her status and has to deal with a hostile Band Council and a vast bureaucracy in Ottawa. Indeed the complexity of the case is further compounded by government departments.

Cecilia Pronovost, a separated mother of six, was born a status Indian at Caughnawaga Reserve near Montreal. She was adopted according to Indian custom and brought up by her granduncle John Charlie and his wife in their home with the daughter of John Charlie and the biological son of Mr. and Mrs. Charlie. John Charlie made a will bequeathing his property and money to his two adopted daughters and cutting off his natural son with $1 "for reasons well known to him." The will also stated that his wife should "have the right of occupancy as long as she lives."[26]

John Charlie died on July 3, 1974, and the will was approved by the Department of Indian Affairs on April 5, 1975.[27] The Department then transferred the property to the wife, Margaret Charlie, on May 7, 1975, a step which does not seem to be in accordance with the terms of the will.[28]

Margaret Charlie was at that time in a hospital which she did not leave until she died one and a half years later on December 28, 1976, without leaving a will.[29]

Cecilia Pronovost, who had been deserted by her husband, who is not an Indian, went with her six children to live in the house which was then claimed by the natural son, John. His stand was supported by the Band Council, who ordered her to vacate the house and leave the reserve.[30] The water supply for the house was cut off. The Department of Indian Affairs on advice from the Justice Department advised the band that following on a 1948 ruling of a Justice Department official, Deputy Minister Varcoe, Cecilia Pronovost could be declared not to be a beneficiary of John Charlie's estate, the house going to the wife and then the son. A request from Mrs. Pronovost's lawyer to the Department of Justice for information on this vital decision produced this response on August 15, 1977: "It is general departmental policy that legal opinions provided from Department of Justice are for department use only."[31]

Immediately after this, although the case was going through the courts, the Department of Indian Affairs transferred the property to the son, John Charlie, on September 1, 1977.[32]

The Band Council wrote to Mrs. Pronovost stating that this was a family matter and advised Mrs. Pronovost not to make the affair public.[33] The Department of Indian Affairs and the Department of Justice solemnly affirm that the fact that Mrs. Pronovost is an Indian woman who has lost her status through marriage has nothing to do with the case.[34] If one asks the question however, "What would be her position with respect to her inheritance if she had not married or had married a member of the band?", the case takes on a very different complexion. Would the Band Council and the government departments have been able to give the same unqualified support and advice to one registered Indian who is male over another who is female? Would they have considered or applied Varcoe's ruling? Even if the validated will were declared invalid,[35] would she not be entitled to inherit from her mother as an adopted child according to section 48 (4), which states that the property of an Indian dying intestate "shall be distributed subject to the rights of the widow, if any, *per stirpes* among such issue", i.e. among his or her children.

Section 48 (16) also states: "In this section 'child' includes a legally adopted child and a child adopted in accordance with Indian custom." These few facts alone suggest that this ignoring of the rights of Cecilia Pronovost has a lot to do with her loss of Indian status and also demonstrates the complex web of oppression in which such women are caught.

Chapter 13

The Unjust Just Society

The position in which Indian women find themselves today seems to reflect a reversal of earlier attitudes on the part of many status Indians to women who "marry out" — that is, status Indians are now generally believed to endorse the principles which successive governments have so long sought to instill — that women, but not men, who marry non-Indians must be penalized. In order to understand how this strange reversal has occurred, it is necessary to look at certain developments which took place during the 1960s.

The early part of the decade was characterized by a concern for human rights, expressed early on by the enactment of the Canadian Bill of Rights in 1960. This was envisaged as a major piece of human rights legislation, but it would seem that this time it was Diefenbaker and his government who laboured long and who "brought forth a mouse", as subsequent events — and particularly the Lavell case — were to demonstrate. Concern for minority rights also resulted in the extension of the franchise to the Indians in 1960, marking the beginning of a new political awareness for and of Indians. At last, instead of having to funnel all complaints and requests through civil servants, they had some access to the political process.

Nevertheless it is important to note here that many Indians objected strongly to being given the franchise and that these objections were clearly related to the confusion between the franchise — the right to vote — and enfranchisement, and the historically justifiable suspicions of the Indians that this was a trap to deprive Indians of their Indian identity, culture and such rights as they then enjoyed.

A circular distributed at that time by the International Committee of Mohawk Arts and Traditions at St. Regis serves to illustrate some of these suspicions. "When the Indians vote, they can no longer be a Sovereign Nation as they automatically become Canadian citizens and British subjects. . . . The REDMAN is morally obliged not to vote in the federal and provincial elections. . . . It is to be deplored that a covey of irresponsible Redmen, sick with racial inferiority complex, shall flock to the polls and *give up their National Identity and Sovereignty* forever!"[1]

The Hawthorn-Tremblay report published in 1967 cogently summarizes some of the reasons for this confusion:

> "In the first place there was an inevitable verbal confusion between the franchise and enfranchisement. The latter was a process whereby the Indian renounced all aspects of Indian status and became, legally, as other Canadians receiving, among other things, the franchise. This automatically coupled the franchise with loss of Indian status in the minds of many Indians, a price they were unwilling to pay. More generally, the absence of the franchise had historically been explained in terms of its incompatibility with Indian status. The general rule from 1920 until 1950 was that Indian status was compatible with the franchise only as a reward for military service. Until all restrictions were finally removed in 1960 the government consistently coupled the retention of certain privileges founded either on treaty or the Indian Act with exclusion from the franchise."[2]

The conceptual and terminological muddle generated by this confounding of the franchise, enfranchisement, and the retention of treaty rights and the Indian Act is a direct inheritance of previous government policies. And this confusion and the concomitant fear of erosion of Indian rights were another important element in the denial of Indian rights to 'enfranchisable' Indian women in the seventies.

Citizens Plus

The extension of the franchise to Indians did not, as was feared by the Indians, diminish their Indian rights; rather, by conferring on them an important legal capacity enjoyed by other citizens, it began to appear that Indians were moving to a position where they had more rights than other citizens, where they were in fact "citizens plus . . . as charter members of the Canadian community", as the Hawthorn-Tremblay Report which was commissioned by the Department of Indian Affairs in 1964 stated in 1967.[3]

This report, undoubtedly the result of the new parliamentary scrutiny of Indian Affairs, represents the first attempt ever at a thorough and critical examination of the social, economic and political situation of Indians in Canada.

An examination of Department of Indian Affairs administration and policies for Indians was an integral part of the inquiry. The Department, which had for so long ruled unchallenged over Indians, was now politically accountable, and this spotlight, the report suggests, "has often resulted in unfair criticisms of the Indian Affairs Branch and therefore has been partially resented by its personnel."[4]

Nevertheless the authors of the report do firmly criticize previous administrations and policy: "This history of neglect and indifference was closely related to the apolitical context of Indian administration."[5] They document economic, health and educational conditions which were a shocking revelation to most Canadians in 1967.

Two years later the Minister of Indian Affairs, Jean Chrétien, in what came to be called the "White Paper", proposed a new deal for Indians. This policy paper deplored the disadvantaged position of Indians and suggested to remedy this a total revision of the Indian Act and the gradual phasing out of the Department of Indian Affairs over five years; the paper also proposed that there should be increased provincial involvement (which had been suggested in the Hawthorne-Tremblay Report) in the Administration of Indian Affairs. It is significant, if not ominous, in the light of subsequent government reaction to the issue of Indian women's rights, that this paper begins: "To be an Indian is to be a man with all a man's needs and abilities."[6]

Some eighteen meetings on changes to the Act had been held with Indians prior to this proposal. When the Indians were presented with the "White Paper" on June 25, 1969, however, there was an immediate and outright rejection of its content. In the first reaction of June 26th, ten Indian Chiefs from across Canada issued a statement declaring that though they did not question the Minister's "good will" they could only "view this as a policy designed to divest us of our aboriginal, residual and statutory rights. If we accept this policy and in the process lose our rights and our lands, we become willing partners in cultural genocide."[7]

"It is apparent to us," they said, "that while there was a show of consultation, neither the Minister nor his Department really heard and understood the Indian people."[8]

At this time two factors strengthened the Indians' position. First, Indians' aspirations to special rights based on aboriginal rights had been given a strong impetus by the imminent settlement of the Alaska native land claims by the U.S. government. Secondly, the formation of the National Indian Brotherhood with membership limited to status Indians in 1968 also seemed to make for a more united Indian political front than had hitherto been possible. It was ironical, though perhaps inevitable, that successful political cohesion depended on Indian Act categories.

The "White Paper", however, had provided real cause for alarm in that it did indeed seem to attempt to play down treaty rights and deny aboriginal land rights: "These aboriginal claims to land are so general and undefined that it is not realistic to think of them as specific claims capable of remedy except through a policy and program that will end injustice to Indians as members of the Canadian community."[9]

Prime Minister Trudeau fanned the flames by stating two months later in a speech in Vancouver: "But aboriginal rights, this really means saying, 'We were here before you!'. . . Our answer .... is 'no'." He then defended the "White Paper" as an attempt to rescue Indians from "the ghetto in which they live".[10] "Canadians", he said, "were not proud of their treatment of Indians in the past and had no reason to be so", but he promised "We will be just in our time. This is all we can do. We must be just today."[10]

But to the Indians this was not justice and this government was not really saying anything new. The "Just Society" and the policy of "integration" which Prime Minister Trudeau and his government were now espousing were only another formulation of assimilation, which had always been the stated intention of every Canadian government. The difference was that Indians were now determined that they would no longer be dictated to by anyone.

Chapter 14

The Lavell Case and Human Rights

The development of native militancy in the late sixties and early seventies culminated in the Lavell case which came before the Supreme Court of Canada in 1973. The events surrounding this case are crucial to understanding the complex approach of status Indians to Indian women's rights today.

Some space therefore must be devoted here to trying to unravel the sequence of these events and to the analysis of the statements and actions of the central figures, as well as to the judgement itself.

The stand taken by Jeannette Lavell was itself first of all a manifestation of the resurgence of pride in Indian identity. It was an affirmation by an Indian woman of belief in the concept of "citizen plus" and the desirability of retaining Indian status. To pose this case as it has been, as one of Indians' rights v. women's rights, is to assume that all Indians are male.

At the same time, however, as Indians in Canada were beginning to take a strong stand Canadian women were also becoming vociferous and demanding change in discriminatory legislation that affected women. As a result, the Royal Commission on the Status of Women was set up in 1967 to investigate the position of Canadian women and to receive evidence from women from all over Canada. Among this evidence, were several briefs from Indian women who had lost their status through marriage asking for changes in the Indian Act and particularly the sections concerning band membership.[1]

Indian women became more hopeful of change when in 1970 an Indian, Drybones, successfully appealed before the Supreme Court a conviction under section 94 (b) of the Indian Act for being found intoxicated off a reserve on the grounds that such a conviction was racially discriminatory and contrary to section 1 (b) of the Canadian Bill of Rights which states:

"1. It is hereby recognized and declared that in Canada there have existed and shall continue to exist without discrimination by race, national origin, colour, religion or sex the following human rights and fundamental freedoms, namely. . . .

b) the right to equality before the law and protection of the law."[2]

The Canadian Bill of Rights seemed to overrule other Acts in the provision which states that "Every law of Canada shall, unless it is expressly declared by an Act of the Parliament of Canada that it shall operate notwithstanding the Canadian Bill of Rights, be so construed and applied so as not to abrogate, abridge or infringe or to authorize the abrogation, abridgement or infringement of any of the rights or freedoms herein recognized and declared."[3]

Before Drybones only two cases had discussed the effects of the Canadian Bill of Rights at length — Regina v. Gonzales, which also concerned an appeal against the liquor provisions of the Indian Act, and Robertson and Rosetani v. the Queen, which had to do with the Lord's Day Act.[4] The invocation of the Bill of Rights in both cases was unsuccessful.

In the case of Drybones it was clearly demonstrated that an Indian was subject to harsher penalties under the liquor provisions of the Indian Act for being found intoxicated in a public place that a non-Indian under the Liquor Ordinance of the Northwest Territories. The Supreme Court found that section 94 (b) of the Indian Act was rendered inoperative because of the Canadian Bill of Rights.

This was the first time that the Supreme Court had squarely faced the issue of the effects of the Bill of Rights and it did so with some reluctance and even trepidation.[5] The judges were alarmed at the discretion that Parliament seemed to allow the courts. In the context of the Indian Act, where Indians had no political voice and where Superintendents-General had held very wide discretionary powers for more than a century, such timidity seems particularly regrettable.

In legal circles this decision evoked a great deal of interest. Indian groups, however, were not very concerned and, it seems, believed that this was an equitable decision.[6]

In 1970, encouraged by both the Drybones decision and the 1970 Report of the Royal Commission on the Status of Women in Canada which condemned 12 (1) (b) in the Indian Act as discriminatory, Jeannette Lavell, an Ojibwa Indian woman who had married a non-Indian, decided to contest the deletion of her name from the band list. The results of her action were unexpected for all concerned.

The time had at last seemed right for Indian women to take a stand. With hindsight, however, it is evident that the time was not right, and Lavell encountered fierce resistance from both the federal government and Indian associations, both of whom for different reasons saw this as an opportunity to make political gains.

The National Indian Brotherhood was just emerging as a viable political organization and was intensely suspicious of the intentions of the federal government after the 1969 "White Paper" proposals. Harold Cardinal, a twenty-four-year-old Indian politician, had just published "The Unjust Society" deriding the whole government and Trudeau's concept of the "Just Society" in a bitter condemnation of past and present government policy for Indians. Most important, however, for the outcome of events in the Lavell case was that enormous emphasis was laid by Cardinal on the retention intact of the Indian Act — a very strange turn of events to most observers. But Cardinal believed that the Act could be used as a lever to put pressure on the government to accede to Indian demands.[7]

Cardinal was not alone in his bitterness and suspicion of the government's intentions. Dave Courchene, President of the Manitoba Indian Brotherhood, also voiced the same extreme suspicion and hostility in a press release in response to the "White Paper" of 1969: "It seems that government, being aware of the increasing strength and ability of Indian organizations, has decided to move now before they become too difficult to deal with or are able to effectively defend themselves."[8]

In somewhat less intemperate vein, the Treaty Indians of Alberta produced "The Red Paper" in 1970, developing the "citizens plus" concept which had been articulated by the government-sponsored Hawthorn-Tremblay Report. They then delivered it to the Prime Minister and the whole Cabinet in Ottawa. The treaty Indians in their "Red Paper" rejected outright the "White Paper" statement "that the legislative and constitutional bases of discrimination should be removed",[9] asserting that "Retaining the legal status of Indians is necessary if Indians are to be treated justly. Justice requires that the special history, rights and circumstances of the Indian people be recognized."[10]

Very significant here, however, is that they begin by emphasizing that discrimination can be benign or negative; that the intended effect of anti-discriminatory legislation is equality and that giving special treatment to some groups is sometimes necessary to achieve "an equilibrium in different situations".[11] This is positive discrimination. Fundamental to this was the retention of the separate Indian status which arose from aboriginal rights in the land.

The government jettisoned its policy paper. But it is clear in retrospect that the "White Paper" had performed a useful function for the Indians in that it had served to raise a national Indian political consciousness by polarizing native opinion against the government. This then seemed to provide a basis for unified action on land claims, which were assuming a new and increasingly dominant position.

Some of the intensity of the subsequent opposition to Lavell and Indian women's rights can fairly be blamed on the "White Paper". But there was more to it than that. The Lavell case appears to have served similar political ends, functioning as a catalyst for both government and Indian political action.

Jeannette Lavell had lost her status on marrying a non-Indian in 1970. She had appealed the decision to delete her name from the Indian register on the basis that it contravened the Bill of Rights. Judge Grossberg was designated under the Indian Act to hear the appeal. Her appeal was dismissed in June 1971. Judge Grossberg evidently believed that Indians themselves had devised the Indian Act and that sex discrimination was not always offensive to the Bill of Rights. He said, "Indians themselves have the capacity and intelligence to judge what is good for them", and that he could not conclude that "inequality within a group or class by itself, by reason of sex, is necessarily offensive to the Bill of Rights."[12]

Jeannette Lavell herself says that Judge Grossberg did not understand why she wished to retain her Indian status and she describes the events thus: "He believed I was better off marrying a white man. In fact according to his readings this was the thinking of all intelligent native people . . ."[13] Subsequently, she writes, "At the Federal Court of Appeal there was no question about it, all three judges felt that I was being discriminated against as this particular section of the Indian Act applied only to Indian women and not Indian men. The Attorney-General's department appealed my victory to the Supreme Court of Canada, no doubt due to pressure from the Department of Indian Affairs and Northern Development and, sad to say, I lost by one vote . . . Not only was this a legal loss but I felt it was also contrary to our traditional values of recognition and respect for each other."[14]

When Lavell won her case at the federal court of appeal in October 1971, another Indian woman who had also lost her Indian status, Yvonne Bedard, appealed successfully in the Supreme Court of Ontario against the action of the Six Nations Council who were evicting her from the reserve despite the fact that the house which she and her children occupied had been willed to her by her mother and that she was separated from her husband.[15]

The two cases of Lavell and Bedard were then appealed and heard together in the Supreme Court of Canada.[16]

The sequence of events and the marshalling of Indian groups against Lavell and Bedard between the Federal Court decision and the Supreme Court proceedings are not at all clear.

The Minister of Indian Affairs of the time, Jean Chrétien, was quoted as being extremely willing to support any Indian band who wished to contest the case.[17] Jeannette Lavell evidently believes that the impetus for contesting the decision of the Federal Court in her favour came from government. Whether this is so or not, lawyers believe that the Attorney-General was bound to bring the matter before the Supreme Court.[18]

However, this is not necessarily the case since the government has refused to proceed to the Supreme Court for almost three years now on cases involving evictions of Indian women from reserves.[19] The political context is clearly important.

Harold Cardinal, then President of the Indian Association of Alberta, continued to organize Indian political activity in the West and kept a high profile by publicly accusing the Minister, Jean Chrétien, of conducting a personal vendetta against him.[20]

Cardinal implies that Chrétien at that time felt that his political credibility if not future was at stake,[21] and it seems both were using the Indian Act as a bargaining tool, but it is evident that if the Indians felt that the Indian Act was a "lever" for them, more than 100 years of experience had proven that it was a stronger lever for the federal government.

Nevertheless the Indians did not all oppose Lavell and there was no agreement at the National Indian Brotherhood Conference in Edmonton in August 1972. The Indian Association of Alberta was therefore forced to go ahead alone, only later being joined by the Indians of Quebec, the Federation of Saskatchewan Indians and then the National Indian Brotherhood.[22] Earlier, the Association of Iroquois and Allied Indians, representing 20,000 Indian men, had asked the government to intervene in the Supreme Court.[23]

Cardinal, in his latest publication, "The Rebirth of Canada's Indians", describes the whole matter in some detail: "We had a tough time controlling those passions and keeping our people focused on the position that whatever injustices an Indian woman faces under the current provisions of the Indian Act can best be rectified when the Indian Act is amended. We fully admitted that such a step was still down the road a way . . ."[24] Cardinal might have thought differently had he been born female. As it was, he evidently felt no compunction in using Indian women as pawns in a power game in which he personally had nothing to lose. If Lavell lost, however, he would hold an even more visibly embarrassing "lever" to force change in the New Indian Act. George Manuel, first President of the NIB, wrote at this time, "There is no doubt that the provision [12 (1) (b)] is unjust in many ways, yet we cannot accept a position where the only safeguards we have had can be struck down by a court that has no authority to put something better in its place. The tragedy of this situation, like so many others, is that it never needed to arise."[25]

The courts it seems took heed of that line of reasoning and did not look separately at the issue of sex discrimination in a particularly unjust section of the Act, as they had done in the Drybones case with race.

In any case, the intervention of the Attorney-General of Canada on behalf of the Indian groups opposing Lavell changed former indecision and confusion into organized confrontation of Indian against Indian in the inexorable process of the law.[26]

In February 1973 the Supreme Court of Canada heard together the cases of Jeannette Lavell and Yvonne Bedard. Their argument was eloquent in its simplicity: that the Indian Act discriminated against them on the basis of race and sex and that, following on the precedent set by Drybones, the Bill of Rights prohibiting such discrimination should override the sections of the Indian Act which discriminated against them as Indian women.[27]

The main thrust of the opposition arguments contained in several facta, and prepared with all the many resources that only government can muster, was 1) that the Indian Act could not be overruled by the Bill of Rights, since the Indian Act had special status as protective legislation under the B.N.A. Act and could not be altered by a court but only by Parliament; 2) that the Indian Act does not discriminate against women; and 3) is merely a legislative embodiment of customary social and economic patterns.[28]

By a five to four decision the Supreme Court judges ruled against Lavell and Bedard, the majority of the Court holding

"1) That the Bill of Rights is not effective to render inoperative legislation such as 12 (1) (b) of the Indian Act passed by the Parliament of Canada in discharge of its Constitutional function under S. 91 (24) of the B.N.A. Act, to specify how and by whom Crown lands reserved by Indians are to be used;

"2) That the *Bill of Rights* does not require federal legislation to be declared inoperative unless it offends against one of the rights specifically guaranteed by section 1, but where legislation is found to be discriminatory, this affords an added reason for rendering it ineffective;

"3) That equality before the law under the Bill of Rights means equality of treatment in the enforcement and application of the laws of Canada before the law enforcement authorities and the ordinary courts of the land, and no such inequality is necessarily entailed in the construction and application of S. 12 (1) (b)."[29]

There has been a great deal of discussion about what this judgement really means. But most authorities seem to agree that reason number one states that the Bill of Rights does not take precedence over the Indian Act.

Law Professor Walter Tarnopolsky finds however that this is beside the point, that it is "an argument both unnecessary and misleadingly prejudicial to a sensible construction of the pertinent subsection of one section of the Indian Act. This was not the issue in Drybones, nor was it the issue in Lavell."[30]

Reason number two (following Tarnopolsky) has to do with the constitutional authority of Parliament mentioned in the preamble to the Bill of Rights, but again this has been variously interpreted and it does not seem useful here to go into this further.

Reason number three has to do with the issue of "equality before the law" which is construed narrowly as meaning "equality in the administration or enforcement of the law" according to Tarnopolsky, not, as it is usually thought, that all persons no matter who they are will be treated as having equal rights before the law.[31]

Drybones, Justice Ritchie argued, was accused of an offence and the Drybones case is thus different from the Lavell case. Justice Ritchie finds in his final statement that the Drybones case was fundamentally different in that it concerned racial discrimination, "whereas no such inequality of treatment between Indian men and women flows as a necessary result of the application of S.112(1)(b) of the Indian Act."[32] This means that within the Indian group Indian women are not discriminated against before the courts or in the administration of the law. There is no explanation of this statement. But it is patently not true since Indian men do not lose their Indian status on marriage to a non-Indian; indeed their wives become Indians, and Indian women (and their subsequent children) do lose their Indian status on marriage to a non-Indian and are forced to give up any inherited property on the reserve, as did Yvonne Bedard. The law is therefore administered differently and deals unequally with Indian women and Indian men. It is very hard to comprehend the logic of this statement of Justice Ritchie, though it should be noted that the Attorney-General's factum argued (it would seem) along the same lines — that Indian women have a "free choice" as to whom they should marry.

The argument that women are discriminated against on the basis of race and sex is thus completely set aside in the majority verdict.[33]

Judge Laskin however, dissenting, states unequivocably that the gist of the judgement in Drybones lay not on the fact that there was a punishable offence involved but "that a legal disability was imposed on a person by reason of his race when other persons were under no similar restraints." He says, "if 'sex' is substituted here for 'race' the result must surely be the same." The fact that it is the Indian Act which specifies discrimination by reason of sex is no argument since the Indian Act is subject as a law of Canada to the Canadian Bill of Rights.

The Indian Act, Laskin says, creates an invidious distinction between brothers and sisters in providing "statutory banishment"[34] for a woman who marries a non-Indian. He adds, "It was urged, in reliance in part on history, that the discrimination embodied in the Indian Act under section 12(1)(b) is based upon a reasonable classification of Indians as a race, that the paramount purpose of the Act to preserve and protect the members of the race is promoted by the statutory preference for Indian men."[35] Apart from the provisions of the Bill of Rights, he says, "I doubt whether discrimination on account of sex where as here it has no biological or physiological rationale could be sustained as a reasonable classification."[36] Indian women, in other words, are no less or no more Indian by reason of sex and their children are genetically as much 'Indian' if they marry a non-Indian as those of a male Indian who marries a non-Indian.

D. V. Smiley, an eminent political scientist, in discussing the Canadian courts and human rights in 1969 made this comment, which seems very appropriate here:

"In ordering the relations between the Canadian Indian and the rest of the community the public authorities need the most sophisticated analyses that social scientists can provide. The Canadian judiciary is badly equipped both by its traditional procedures and by training and inclination to use scientific knowledge creatively in the making of public policy. The legal realists [as opposed to the positivists] assert that the courts in coming to decisions do in fact take into account a broader range of factors than the canons of statutory interpretation imply. Particularly in a review of the constitution, where the range of constitutional discussion is often wider than when other statutes are involved, it is inevitable that judges will be influenced by the formulations of the essential nature of the policy and their evaluations of the public consequences of their decisions. However, within the Canadian tradition these considerations are seldom made explicit and are concealed in decisions within a mass of legal verbiage unintelligible to the average interested citizen."[37]

The decision in the Lavell case was indeed puzzling. None of the major issues involved were resolved. Nevertheless the consequences of the decision for Indian women were serious, since they were left with no route of appeal but Parliament and they were politically powerless. Perhaps it is a result of the fact that Indian women have for so long been deprived in law of a political voice that so many otherwise well-informed commentators on this case endorse the present system of status determination as an embodiment of native custom and a tenable argument since it prevents demographic distortions.[38]

And this viewpoint, with its implicit acceptance of benevolent paternalism as a past government policy, was advanced in the historical arguments made in the court that the purpose of the Act was to "preserve and protect" and that the classification followed custom.[39] These arguments were influential in the judgements, as Laskin noted.[40]

The factum of the Attorney-General, for example, begins by stating that the Act presents a comprehensive legislative scheme "devised for the welfare of the Indians in Canada. Under its provisions Indians are subject to a legal regime peculiar to them but apparently deemed necessary and desirable having regard to the historical development and circumstances of this particular group of persons."[41] The factum goes on, "The policy behind the statute is probably reflected by the following statement . . . to the Prime Minister . . . in June 1970 by the Indian Chiefs of Alberta. 'Retaining the legal status of Indians is necessary if Indians are to be treated justly. Justice requires that the special history, rights and circumstances of Indian People be recognized'."

It is extremely unlikely that any of those chiefs thought that their statement would be construed so as to endorse the Indian Act. In addition, the Attorney-General confuses the Act and treaty rights, whether intentionally or not, and reinforces the Harold Cardinal "lever" strategy as well as reiterating the myth already repudiated by Prime Minister Trudeau and his government that past treatment of Indians had been something Canadians should be proud of.

As has been shown in this study, the welfare of the Indians was not at any time the main basis of Indian policy. Attitudes to Indians and the policies and legislation codified in the later nineteenth century legislation did not represent the wishes or customs of Indians and are characterized primarily by self-interest. This was entirely consistent with most of nineteenth-century philosophy and ethics.

The argument offered by the factum of the Council of the Six Nations, which states that the Act was the legislative embodiment of Indian custom, is also erroneous. There was prior to the Act of 1869 considerable heterogeneity in Indian customs across Canada as to kinship, marriage, descent and residence patterns. Patrilineal descent and patrilocal residence were not the rule everywhere or even perhaps anywhere. This factum emphasized that the purpose of the 1869 legislation was to protect Indians from the white men who married Indian women.[42]

The implication of inevitable white male superiority held by most non-Indans is still an integral premise of the same much iterated argument, that if Indian women are allowed to retain Indian status on marrying white men, these men will take over the reserve. This is an argument which seems to reflect the powerful role of government and the white Indian Agent on the reserve more than anything else. Since this argument implies white superiority, it is an argument which is manifestly acceptable to, and fostered perhaps unconsciously by, many white men. But since most, if not all, of the evictions from reserves concern old women, widows and separated women, this has obviously little to do with the situation today.[43]

The Canadian sociologist Frideres has stated that this argument seems "naive" and self-serving. In the U.S., he notes, any Indian woman may marry whom she pleases and retain her status and name on the list of members while "the spouse retains her ethnic classification but the offspring must apply for Indian status. The results show that their reserves have not been taken over by whites."[44]

Another aspect of this often repeated argument, which endorses the double standard between Indian men and Indian women, is implicit in the following excerpt from the life history of an Ojibwa Indian woman, Verna Johnston.

> "Those 'half-breeds' who were the children of white fathers and Indian mothers learned Ojibwa as their first language, and this seems to have pushed all of them in the direction of Indian identity, rather than white or dual. Verna and her siblings and cousins were children of white mothers, and many more of them chose to emphasize the white or the dual aspects of their identity."[45]

It is the mother, this suggests, who is mainly responsible for transmitting cultural identity.

Confusion has always existed between the legal, ethnic and biological distinctions in the Indian Act (and with good reason). This confusion is shared by Indians and non-Indians alike. The outcome of the Lavell case was to contribute substantially to this, by the apparent endorsement of the arguments made by those opposing Lavell, since Lavell was unsuccessful, as much as by the decision of the majority of the court.

Chapter 15

The Resolution of the Problem?

Many parliamentarians are beginning to find the legislation on Indian women an embarrassing anachronism, especially since the issue of loss of status is now being clearly seen as a violation of fundamental human rights.

Unfortunately, they now are hoist with their own petard and believe they cannot act contrary to what seem to be the wishes of the political voice of Indians, the NIB.

The joint National Indian Brotherhood-Cabinet Committee to revise the Indian Act, set up in 1975, has so far met three times. The government promised the NIB not to make any changes to the Act until the whole Act is revised.[1] Most indications are that this is not even on the horizon.[2] Two sub-committees have been established to discuss land claims and the Indian Act and research teams are studying these. Membership is not one of the topics for which a sub-committee has been set up and had not been proposed as a topic for discussion before December of 1977. According to Noel Starblanket this is because "the whole question of membership is so complicated".[3]

In September 1977, when the research for this study was begun, the view was frequently expressed in interviews with civil servants in the Department of Indian Affairs that even to research the issue was liable to upset the delicately balanced negotiations between government and the NIB. Thus it seems the rationale used by Cardinal which justified the victimization of Indian women has become conventional wisdom.

One partial explanation for the present NIB stance is, it would seem, that the representatives of the "treaty" Indians on the NIB board still believe that the Cardinal strategy and values are valid.

Since November 1977, however, a change of mood appears to have occurred and a more favorable attitude towards the issue has developed. The unmitigating efforts of the national association of Indian Rights for Indian Women have undoubtedly played a major role. There is a realization also by politicians that the Indian women will not be silenced and that this is politically embarrassing and an indefensible position for a government just enacting a new Human Rights Act.[4]

The continuing efforts of Canadian women's groups such as the

Federal Advisory Council on the Status of Women and the National Action Committee to prevent the Indian women's protests from being stifled have also been significant.

Statements made by Noel Starblanket, President of the National Indian Brotherhood, in October 1977, promising his support to the women, gave "respectability" to the issue in the eyes of many — if only temporarily.[5]

Clearly it will be rather difficult now for Indian politicians to change their minds on a strategy which may have outlived its usefulness but which appeared to be very successful and has now achieved the force of dogma. Nevertheless it is surely apparent that if the NIB is not seen to represent its constituents it will not survive as the powerful national body negotiating for all Indians which it is today.

Its constituents comprise also "non-treaty" Indians and these "non-treaty" Indians as well as the Inuit and Métis, who are presently involved in submitting land claims to the government, do not discriminate against women where they include a provision on eligibility or membership.

In the James Bay and northern Quebec agreement for example, eligibility criteria for the Cree depend primarily on recognition by the community and residence, and include illegitimate and adopted children. No distinction is made between men and women and eligibility is extended to persons "of Cree ancestry ordinarily resident in the Territory".[6] Definitions established by the Inuit for their claims are similar, except that these also include "the lawful spouse" of a person considered to be eligible as a beneficiary.[7]

The eligibility or membership proposals of the Yukon Indian Claim, Document #3, March 8, 1977 are slightly different but also very broad, emphasizing one-quarter Indian blood and the right of the community to decide on membership.[8] Again, no distinction is made between men and women.

The Indian Brotherhood of the Northwest Territories state, "The definition of the Dene is the right of the Dene. The Dene know who they are."[9] The Métis Association of the Northwest Territories in their claim state, "It is generally agreed that the right to decide who belongs to a group is the right of the group to decide".[10]

What all these criteria cited by the different native groups have in common is that 1) the native group will decide on membership; 2) residence criteria are important; and occasionally 3) a one-quarter "blood" requirement. All these are much broader and more inclusive than the membership provisions of the Indian Act, women and men are treated equally, and illegitimate birth is not an issue.

In 1974 the Report of the Indian Act Study Team prepared for the NIB recommended that discrimination against Indian women be removed from the Act and that Indian women should not lose status on marriage. The non-Indian spouses of Indians and their children would not acquire status. This would certainly have significant effects in limiting the size of the status Indian population.[11]

But since the articulation of the special status concept "citizens plus", Indian leaders have continued to insist that section 12(1)(b) must not be repealed, however unjust (and the leaders at least all agree that it is). They claim that the Indian Act, which symbolizes their special status, will be thus laid open to government attempts to encroach on this special status. It appears that some also believe that such sections in the Act as those which deprive Indian women of their rights are such embarrassing anachronisms that they can be used as a lever by the NIB in the joint negotiations.

The NIB in the present joint government-Indian negotiations to revise the Indian Act has refused to allow status or non-status native women's organizations to be represented in these negotiations. Curiously the federal government does not see anything at all amiss with the fact that the NIB can unilaterally make such a decision. As "Indians" meant only males to the governments in the past, so it is today.[12]

The government also believes that it can escape the consequences of confronting the issue by laying the whole blame for the continuing discrimination on the NIB, by arguing that it has promised the NIB not to make any changes to the Indian Act until the whole Act is revised through the joint NIB-government committee, and that any interim attempts to alleviate the women's situation would be interpreted as bad faith.[13]

This denial of the human rights of Indian women on the part of both the government and the NIB has been compounded by the fact that this same government has carefully excluded any possible recourse in law by removing the Indian Act from the reach of the new Human Rights Act[14] which came into force on March 1, 1978. Indian women have nowhere to turn and are denied the basic human rights enjoyed by other Canadians.

The Minister of Justice, in an attempt to explain this policy, said that because of the joint consultative process with the NIB to revise the Indian Act, he had no alternative but to exclude it.[15]

Neither of the two main Indian women's groups, the Native Women's Association (composed of both status and non-status women) or the National Association of Indian Rights for Indian Women, has been permitted to take part in this joint consultative process. As recently as December 12, 1977, despite Noel Starblanket's commitment, the executive council of the NIB refused to consider allowing representatives from either of these national native women's groups to take part in the consultations.[16]

At the time of the Lavell case there were no women on the National Indian Brotherhood executive council and the Iroquois and Allied Indian group, who first enlisted the help of the Solicitor-General and turned the tide against Lavell, represented 20,000 Indian men.[17] At present (February 1978) the Indian Brotherhood executive council has eleven members, none of whom are women. At the September 1977 annual NIB conference, out of 68 delegates only one was a woman (from B.C.).[18]

Indian Rights for Indian Women is at present considering options for a definition of membership which would replace the present discriminatory sections of the Indian Act. Their work is complicated by the fact that neither Indian women nor Indian men have much knowledge of the contents of the Indian Act, if indeed they have heard of it at all. Even if they possess a copy of it, it is phrased in tortuous English which is very difficult to understand even if one's first language is English. The research at present almost completed in Alberta by IRIW and the report of research conducted by the Quebec Native Woman Association, entitled "Wake Up Native Women", in the summer of 1977, clearly substantiate this. From 435 questionnaires administered by six native women researchers it was found that 49% of both men and women had never heard of the Indian Act. Of the 51% who had, less than half had ever read the Act. Sixty-one percent of the native people interviewed had a relative or close friend who had lost his or her Indian status and 86% of these were through marriage.[19] Only 16% agreed with the present method of according status only through the male.[20]

What is especially noteworthy about these findings is that a good cross-section of Indians from Quebec were interviewed and the results strongly contradict the stand taken by the band chiefs from the reserves in southern Quebec (Caughnawaga and St. Regis), who are said to be most influential in the joint NIB-government Indian Act revisions.[21]

As an interim measure, Indian Rights for Indian Women has made three minimal requests to government to alleviate the situation in which Indian women now find themselves.[22]

They have asked that evictions of Indian women and children from reserves be stopped immediately. Those who are being evicted are elderly women, widows and deserted mothers with small children. This request, however, has been rejected.

IRIW have asked that since both government and Indian leaders have said that 12(1)(b) is unjust and discriminatory the implementation of this section be suspended until the whole Act is revised. This request has also been denied.

They have asked that, since it is their fate that is being decided and Indian women are at least half of the Indian population, Indian women's organizations be allowed an official voice in the representation in the joint NIB-government negotiations to make revisions to the Indian Act. This request also has been refused.

One thing is clear — that to be born poor, an Indian and a female is to be a member of the most disadvantaged minority in Canada today, a citizen minus. It is to be victimized and utterly powerless and to be, by government decree, without legal recourse of any kind.

Specimen Calculation — per capita share of oil and gas royalties

Example: Reserve X, Alberta   Pop. 3,000
Sources: R. G. McCrossan. The Future Petroleum Provinces of Canada, 1973. P. Van Meurs & Associates.

Alberta

Total area of oil and gas bearing territory
(Craton Margin) = 113,000 sq. miles
Ultimate recoverable potential oil = 13.7 billion barrels
Ultimate recoverable potential gas = 65.6 trillion cu. ft.
∴ Approximate recoverable oil per sq. mile = 121,000 barrels
∴ Approximate recoverable gas per sq. mile = 580 million cu. feet

Reserve X

Area of Reserve X = 160 sq. miles
∴ Average potential reserve of soil = 121,000 x 160
= 19.3 million barrels
∴ Average potential reserve of gas = 580,000,000 x 160
= 93 billion cu. feet
Population of Reserve X = ±3,000
∴ Reserve of oil per capita = 6,400 barrels
∴ Reserve of gas per capita = 30 million cu. feet

Royalty value per person in Reserve X

Assume royalty = ⅓ gross value of
$10 per barrel of oil
$ 1 per thousand cu. ft. of gas
∴ Royalty value per person for oil and gas
= ⅓ [10 x 6400 + 1 x 30,000]
= ±$31,000

Assume $1000 per year equal payments over 31 years and apply escalation of 11% in current dollars which includes 6% inflation.

Then Discounted Cash Flow (DCF) at 5% discount rate in current dollars.

Once for all cash payment = $15,000

References

P.A.C. — Public Archives of Canada.

Chapter 1

[1]Indian Act, R.S.C. 1970, c.I-6.

[2]Two-Axe Early, Mary, and Ross, Philomena, *Minutes of Proceedings and Evidence of the Standing Committee on Indian Affairs and Northern Development* (Issue No. 53, May 25, 1956), p. 12, p. 23.

[3]*Citizenship Act*. R.S., c. 33, s. 1 (1977).

[4]These comments are based on interviews with IRIW members, Noel Starblanket, President of NIB, and federal government officials, September-November 1977.

[5]Chrétien, Hon. Jean, *Indian Policy, Statement of the Government of Canada* (Ottawa, 1969). Afterwards called the "White Paper".

[6]Cardinal, Harold, *The Unjust Society* (Edmonton: M. G. Hurtig, 1961), p. 140.

[7]Drake, St. Clair, "The Social and Economic Status of the Negro in the United States", in A. Béteille, ed., *Social Inequality* (Harmondsworth: Penguin, 1969) p. 299.

[8]*Canadian Human Rights Act, 1976-77.*

[9]Manuel, George, *The Fourth World* (New York: The Free Press, 1974), p. 241, and Cardinal, Harold, *The Rebirth of Canada's Indians* (Edmonton: Hurtig, 1977), p. 110-113.

[10]*The Globe and Mail,* May 26, 1977.

[11]*The Globe and Mail,* February 17, 1978.

[12]Starblanket, Noel, speech to National Conference of IRIW, October 22, 1978, and interview with Advisory Council on the Status of Women, November 2, 1978.

[13]Sickels, Robert J., *Race, Marriage and the Law* (Albuquerque: University of New Mexico Press, 1972):
Despite the apparent receptiveness of the U.S. Supreme Court to complaints of unequal treatment under the law after the gain for racial equality made in Brown v. The Board of Education in 1954 the Supreme Court consistently avoided facing the main issue in appeals against convictions for mixed marriages which could range from a fine up to several years in jail. It was not until many other decisions on racial equality had rendered this a non-issue that in 1967 (Loving v. Virginia) laws in 16 states banning interracial marriage were declared unconstitutional.

Chapter 2

[1]*Indian Act,* R.S.C. 1970, C.I-6.s.11.

[2]Ibid., s.12(1)(b).

[3]Ibid., s.12(2).

[4]*An Act for the better protection of Lands and Property of the Indians in Lower Canada,* s.c. 1850, c. 42, and *An Act for the protection of Indians in Upper Canada from imposition and the property occupied or enjoyed by them from trespass and injury,* s.c. 1850, c. 74, were the first Acts for Indians of general application.

Ordinances and Acts legislating for specific groups were made from 1763 on, however.

[5]*An Act for the gradual enfranchisement of Indians, the better management of Indian Affairs, and to extend the provisions of the Act 31st Victoria, Chapter 42,* s.c. 1869, c. 6.

[6] *An Act to amend certain Laws respecting Indians and to extend certain Laws relating to matters connected with Indians to the Provinces of Manitoba and British Columbia,* s.c. 1874, c. 21.

[7]Cumming, Peter A., and Mickenberg, Neil H., *Native Rights in Canada,* 2nd ed. (Toronto: Indian-Eskimo Association of Canada, 1972), p. 75-80.

[8]Ibid., p. 69, p. 82-83.

[9]A large bark or skin covered lodge in which several nuclear families lived.

[10]Driver, A. H., *Indians of North America,* 2nd ed. (Chicago: University of Chicago Press, 1969), p. 231, 246, 278.

[11]Goldenweiser, Alexander A., *On Iroquois Work, 1912* and *On Iroquois Work, 1913-1914* (1912, 1914), cited in Brown, Judith K., "Iroquois Women: An Ethnohistoric Note" in Reiter, Rayna R., ed., *Toward an Anthropology of Women* (New York: Monthly Review Press, 1975), p. 239.

[12]Schoolcraft, Henry R., *Notes on the Iroquois* (1847) (1860), cited in Brown, Judith K., op. cit., p. 239.

[13]Lafitau, Joseph F., *Moeurs des sauvages amériquains, comparées au moeurs des premiers temps,* cited in Brown, Judith K., op. cit., p. 238.

[14]Brown, Judith K., op. cit., p. 251.

[15]Rowbotham, Sheila, *Hidden from History* (London: Pluto Press, 1973), p. 47.

[16]Ibid., p. 58-59.

[17]Steward, Julian H., "The economic and social basis of primitive bands", in Lowie, R. H., ed., *Essays in Anthropology presented to A. L. Kroeber* (Berkeley: University of California Press, 1936).

[18]Service, Elman, *Primitive Social Organization: an evolutionary perspective* (New York: Random House, 1962), p. 65-67, p. 107-109.

[19]Radcliffe-Brown, A. R., *Social Organization of Australian Tribes* (Oceania Monographs 1), p. 35.

[20]Lee, Richard B., and Devore, Irven, eds, *Man the Hunter* (Chicago: Aldine Publishing Company, 1968), p. 7-8.

[21]Ibid., p. 7.

[22]Leacock, Eleanor, "The Montagnais-Naskapi Band", in Cox, Bruce, ed., *Cultural Ecology* (Toronto: McClelland and Stewart, 1973), p. 86.

[23]Martin, Kay, *The Foraging Adaptation — Uniformity or Diversity* (Addison-Wesley Module no. 56, 1974), p. 30.

[24]Samuelson, Paul Anthony, *Economics,* 10th ed. (New York: McGraw-Hill, 1976).

[25]Sanday, Peggy, "Toward a Theory of the Status of Women", *American Anthropologist* (1975), p. 1682-1700.

[26]Bamberger, Joan, "The Myth of Matriarchy", in Rosaldo, M. Z., and Lamphere, L., eds., *Woman, Culture and Society* (Stanford: Stanford University Press, 1974), p. 263-280. Sacks, Karen, "Engels Revisited", in Rosaldo and Lamphere, eds, op. cit., p. 207-222, provides background to this.

[27]Rowbotham, Sheila, op. cit., also Bridenthal, Renate, and Koonz, Claudia, eds., *Becoming Visible: Women in European History* (Boston: Houghton Mifflin, 1977).

[28]See p. 51 and p. 109 in this study.

[29]Acton, Janice, Goldsmith, P., and Shepard, B., eds., *Women at Work, Ontario 1850-1930* (Toronto: Canadian Women's Educational Press, 1974) contains several articles on this topic. Also Millet, Kate, *Sexual Politics* (New York: Doubleday, 1969), p. 68.

Chapter 3

[1]Jaenen, Cornelius J., *Friend & Foe* (Toronto: McClelland and Stewart, 1976), p. 153.

[2]Rich, E. E. *The Hudson's Bay Company, 1660-1870,* 3 volumes (New York: Macmillan, 1961).

[3]Giraud, Marcel, *Le Métis Canadien* (Paris, 1945), p. 308.

[4]Jaenen, Cornelius J., op. cit., p. 163.

[5]Ibid., p. 164-165.

[6]Brown, Jennifer, "Fur Traders Racial Categories, and Kinship Networks", in *Papers of the Sixth Algonquian Conference, 1974* (Ottawa: National Museums of Canada, 1975), p. 217.

[7]Jaenen, Cornelius J., op. cit., p. 175.

[8]Ibid., p. 177-178.

[9]Cumming, Peter A., and Mickenberg, Neil H., *Native Rights in Canada,* 2nd ed. (Toronto: Indian-Eskimo Association of Canada, 1970), p. 79-80.

[10]Rich, E. E., *The Fur Trade and the North West to 1857* (Toronto: McClelland and Stewart, 1967), Chapters 1-6.

[11]Rich, E. E., op. cit., p. 145, 496.

[12]Van Kirk, Sylvia, "The Custom of the Country — An Examination of Fur Trade Marriage Practices", in Thomas, L. H., ed., *Essays in Western History* (Edmonton: University of Alberta Press, 1976).

[13]Brown, Jennifer, op. cit., p. 217.

[14]Van Kirk, Sylvia, op. cit., p. 50.

[15]Van Kirk, Sylvia, op. cit., p. 50-51.

[16]Jamieson, K., and Cox, Bruce, "Indian-White Marriage in Canada, an analysis of three court cases" (paper read at Annual Conference of American Society for Ethnohistory, Chicago, 1977), p. 10.

[17]*Johnstone et al. vs. Connolly,* Court of Appeal, 7 September 1869 (cited in *La Revue légale* I, p. 253-400).

[18]Sanders, Douglas, "Family Law and Native People" (unpublished paper for the Law Reform Commission of Canada, 1975), p. 51.

[19]*Johnstone et al. vs. Connolly,* op. cit.

[20]Brown, Jennifer, op. cit., p. 64.

[21]Van Kirk, Sylvia, op. cit., p. 61.

[22]Simpson, George, *Journals* (1968), p. 58.

[23]Van Kirk, Sylvia, "Women and the Fur Trade", *Beaver* (Winter, 1972), p. 10-11.

[24]Bolt, Christine, *Victorian Attitudes to Race* (London: Routledge & Kegan Paul, 1971), extensive background.

[25]Van Kirk, Sylvia, op. cit., p. 13-14.

[26]Foster, John, "The Origins of the Mixed Bloods in the Canadian West", in Thomas, L. G., ed., op. cit., p. 76. The two papers by Sylvia Van Kirk cited above are also relevant here.

[27]Surtees, R. J., "The Development of an Indian Reserve Policy in Canada", in Johnson, J. K., ed., *Historical Essays on Upper Canada* (Toronto: McClelland and Stewart, 1975).

[28]Surtees, R. J., Ibid., p. 252.

[29]Ibid., p. 267.

[30]*Constitutional Documents,* 1759-1791, Vol. 1, pt. 1. *Sessional Papers,* No. 18, 1907.

[31]Ibid.

[32]Surtees, R. J., op. cit., p. 265.

[33]*Annual Reports 1838-46* and *Transactions of the Aborigines Protection Society* 1839-1907 (British Library), p. 1017, 1019.

[34]Darling to Dalhousie, July 24, 1828 (Parliamentary Papers No. 617).

Chapter 4

[1]Surtees, R.J., op. cit., p. 268-274.

[2]Ibid.

[3]Cumming, Peter A., and Mickenberg, Neil H., op. cit., p. 113-114.

[4]Surtees, R. J., *Indian Reserve Policy in Upper Canada, 1830-1847* (M.A. thesis, Carleton University, 1966), p. 42.

[5]Cumming, Peter A., and Mickenberg, Neil H., op. cit., p. 114.

[6]Ibid., p. 114.

[7]Surtees, R. J., op. cit., p. 139.

[8]*Report on the Affairs of the Indians of Canada,* J.L.A.C. 1844-5, Appendix E.E.E.

[9]Ibid., March 20, 1845.

[10]Ibid.

[11]Peter Jones to Glenelg, J.L.A.C. 1847: App.T.

[12]"Report on the Affairs of the Indians of Canada", op. cit. all subsequent quotations from this report. N.P.

Chapter 5

[1]*An Act to authorize the setting apart of Lands for the use of certain Indian Tribes in Lower Canada,* s.c. 1851, c. 106.

[2]*An Act for the better protection of Lands and Property of the Indians in Lower Canada,* s.c. 1850, c. 42.

[3]*An Act to repeal and in part amend an Act, entitled, An Act for the better protection of the Lands and Property of the Indians in Lower Canada,* s.c. 1851, c. 59.

[4]*An Act for the protection of the Indians in Upper Canada from imposition and the property occupied or enjoyed by them from trespass and injury,* s.c. 1850, c. 74.

[5]Oliphant to Elgin, PAC, Q. Series, Series I, Orders in Council.

[6]Bury to Head, 1855, Ibid.

[7]Head to Labouchère, Ibid.

[8]Labouchère to Head, P.A.C. Q Series, June 2, 1856.

[9]*An Act to encourage the gradual civilization of the Indian Tribes in this Province, and to amend the Laws respecting Indians*, s.c. 1854, c. 26.

[10]Ibid. (Preamble).

[11]Ibid.

[12]Ibid.

[13]*Report of the Special Commissioners to Investigate Indian Affairs in Canada*, J.L.A.C. App. 21.

[14]Ibid.

[15]Ibid.

[16]Ibid.

[17]The British North America Act (U.K.), 30 & 31 Vic. (1867), c. 3.

[18]Cumming, Peter A., and Mickenberg, Neil H., op. cit., p. 6-9.

Chapter 6

[1]*An Act providing for the organization of the Department of Secretary of State of Canada, and for the management of Indian and Ordnance Lands*, s.c. 1868, c. 42.

[2]*An Act for the gradual enfranchisement of Indians, the better management of Indian affairs, and to extend the provisions of the Act 31st Victoria, Chapter 42*, s.c. 1869, c. 6.

[3]PAC, R.G. 10 Red Series, Vol. 1934, 3541.

[4]Zaslow, Morris, *The Opening of the Canadian West, 1870-1914* (Toronto: McClelland and Stewart, 1971), p. 2.

[5]*Commons Debates*, April 27, 1869, p. 83.

[6]Ibid., p. 84.

[7]Ibid., p. 84-85.

[8]Ibid., p. 85.

[9]Ibid., p. 85.

[10]Ibid., p. 84.

[11]The profound and unprecedented changes occurring in Canada at this time no doubt also contributed to this 'adhoc-ery'.

[12]Weaver, Sally M., *Report on Archival Research* (Reasons for introduction of s. 6 into s.c. 1869, c. 6), p. 3.

[13]PAC. R.G. 10. Vol. 527, cited in Weaver, Ibid., p. 12.

[14]Six Nations Council Minutes, January 20, 1870, cited in Weaver, Ibid., p. 19.

[15]Ibid., p. 16.

[16]Ibid., p. 16-17.

[17]Ibid., p. 18-19.

[18]PAC. R.G. 10. Vol. 528, cited in Weaver, Ibid., p. 11.

[19]PAC. R.G. 10. Vol. 857, cited in Weaver, Ibid., p. 12.

[20]*Report of the Indian Branch of the Department of the Secretary of State for the Provinces, for the Year Ending on the 30th June, 1870* (Canada Sessional Papers, 1871, No. 23). p. 5.

[21]Ibid.

[22]Ibid., p. 68.

[23]PAC, R.G. 10, Vol. 723, cited in Weaver, op. cit., p. 13.

[24]*Transactions* of the British and Foreign Aborigines Protection Society, 1859-66, p. 148-158 (British Library, p. 1019).

[25]*Report of the Indian Branch of the Department of the Secretary of State for the Provinces* (Canada Sessional Papers, 1872).

[26]PAC, R. G. 10. Red Series, Vol. 1934, 3541.

Chapter 7

[1]Morris, Alexander, *The Treaties of Canada with the Indians of Manitoba and The North-West Territories* (Toronto: Belfords, Clarke & Co., 1880), p. 183.

[2]In 1978, Robinson Treaty and Treaty 9 paid $4. All other treaties pay $5. See I.A.N.D. Publication No. QS-0454-000-BB-A3.

[3]An Act to amend and continue the Act 32 and 33 Victoria, Chapter 3, and to establish and provide for the Government of the Province of Manitoba, s.c. 1870, c. 3.

[4]Canada Sessional Papers, 1871, No. 20, p. 8.

[5]*Dominion Lands Act,* s.c. 1872, c. 23.

[6]*The Indian Act,* 1876, s.c. 1976, c. 18.

[7]Treaty Nos. 1 & 2, 160 acres per family of five. Treaty No. 3 & 4, 6, 7, 9, 10, 11, up to one square mile per family of five. See I.A.N.D. Publication No. QS-0454-000-BB-A3.

[8]Canada Sessional Papers, 1871, No. 20, p. 8.

[9]Morris, Alexander, op. cit.

[10]Cumming, Peter A., and Mickenberg, Neil H., op. cit., p. 200-207.

[11]Ibid., p. 200.

[12]Cumming, Peter A., and Mickenberg, Neil H., op. cit., p. 200-204.

[13]Morris, Alexander, op. cit., p. 34.

[14]Ibid., p. 35.

[15]Ibid., p. 41.

[16]Ibid., p. 69.

[17]Ibid., p. 98.

[18]Ibid., p. 123.

[19]Ibid., p. 222.

Chapter 8

[1]s.c. 1874, c. 21.

[2]*The Indian Act,* 1876, s.c. 1876, c. 18.

[3]Ibid., s. 3.

[4]*House of Commons Debates,* March 28, 1976.

[5]Membership Division, DIAND — number not known.

[6]*House of Commons Debates,* March 31, 1876.

[7]s.c. 1876, c. 18, s. 86-94.

[8]PAC, R. G. 10, B3, Vol. 6808.

[9]s.c. 1876, c. 18, 3.3(c).

[10]*The Canada Year Book 1948-49,* Government of Canada, Dominion Bureau of Statistics (Ottawa: King's Printer, 1949), p. xvi. In 1871, for example, there were 4 divorces in Canada; in 1881 there were 7 divorces.

[11]*An Act to amend 'The Indian Act, 1876",* s.c. 1879, c. 34.

[12]*The Criminal Code,* s.c. 1892, c. 29, s. 190.

[13]*House of Commons Debates,* May 5, 1880.

[14]*The Indian Act,* s.c. 1880, c. 28, s. 23.

[15]See p. 153.

[16]*Annual Report, 1880,* Canada, Department of Indian Affairs, p. 26.

[17]Ibid., p. 2.

[18]P.A.C. R.G. 10.B & 3, Vol. 4423. Vankoughenet to Agent at Shubenacadie, April 27, 1880.

[19]Stanley, George F. G., *The Birth of Western Canada: A History of the Riel Rebellions* (Toronto: University of Toronto Press, 1960) p. 269-274.

[20]Ibid.

[21]*House of Commons Debates,* March 31, 1879.

[22]Morris, Alexander, op. cit., p. 283.

[23]Ibid., p. 283-284.

[24]Stanley, George F. G., *The Birth of Western Canada: A History of the Riel Rebellions,* reprint (Toronto, 1961).

[25]*The Indian Advancement Act, 1884,* s.c. 1884, c. 28.

[26]*The Indian Advancement Act, 1886,* R.s.c. 1886, c. 44.

[27]*The Electoral Franchise Act,* s.c. 1885, c. 40, s. 11, 64.

[28]*House of Commons Debates,* May 4, 1805.

[29]Hawthorn, H. B., ed., *A Survey of the Contemporary Indians of Canada,* Vol. I (Ottawa: DIAND, 1966), p. 256.

[30]Ibid.

[31]*An Act further to amend "The Indian Act, 1880",* s.c. 1884, c. 27, s. 3.

[32]Ibid., s. 5. "20.(3)".

[33]*The Indian Act,* R.s.c. 1886, c. 43, s. 117.

[34]*An Act to amend "The Indian Act",* s.c. 1887, c. 33, s.1.

[35]*An Act further to amend "The Indian Act",* s.c. 1894, c. 32, s.11.137, 138, ss. 2.

[36]DIAND, *The Historical Development of the Indian Act,* unpublished (1975), p. 105.

[37]*An Act further to amend "The Indian Act",* s.c. 1894, s. 2.

Chapter 9

[1]Raby, Stewart, "Indian Land Surrenders in Southern Saskatchewan", *Canadian Geographer,* XVII: 1 (1973), p. 37-39.

[2]Ibid., p. 37.

[3]*An Act to amend the Indian Act,* s.c. 1911, c. 14, 2. "49A".

[4]Scott to Indian Agents, P.A.C. R.G.10, Vol. 6810, 1913, s. 5.

[5]Ibid., s. 16.

[6]Scott, D. C., "The Indians of Canada Since Confederation", speech, P.A.C. R.G. 10. 577. file 127, 33 vol. 1A.

[7]*An Act to amend the Indian Act,* s.c. 1918, c. 26, 1918, 122A(2).

[8]Ibid., s.c. 1919-20, c. 50.

[9]R.G. 10. Vol. 6810, N-3 1920.

[10]Evidence of D. C. Scott, Ibid.

[11]Manuel, George, and Posluns, Michael, *The Fourth World* (New York: The Free Press, 1974) p. 77.

[12]Tobias, John L., "Protection, Civilization, Assimilation: An Outline History of Canada's Indian Policy", *The Western Canadian Journal of Anthropology,* Vol. VI, No. 2 (1976), p. 23.

[13]Op. cit., s.c. 1919-20, c. 50, 2 "14".

[14]*The Indian Act,* R.S.C. 1927, s. 98.

[15]Ibid., s. 26(d).

[16]Ibid., s. 12.

[17]Ibid., s. 35.

[18]*An Act to amend the Indian Act,* s.c. 1924, c. 47, s. 1(2).

[19]Half-breed Commission Report, Government of Alberta, 1936, Findings cited in *The Metis People of Canada: A History,* Alberta Federation of Metis Settlement Associations (1977), p. 106-107.

[20]*An Act to amend the Indian Act,* s.c. 1930, c. 25, s. 16 "140A".

[21]Scott, Duncan, *The Administration of Indian Affairs in Canada* (Canadian Institute of International Affairs, 1931), p. 25.

[22]Fumoleau, René, op. cit., p. 20.

[23]P.A.C. R.G. 10, Vol. 6813, File 481-1-14, *Policy on Half-breeds* in Saskatchewan and Alberta, 1924-46.

[24]Letter from agent at Hobbema, to Dept. of Mines and Resources, October 5, 1937, op. cit.

[25]Letter from Dept. to Agent, October 26, 1937, op. cit.

[26]P.A.C. R.G. 10, Vol. 6812, File 481-1-14.

[27]P.A.C. R.G. 10, 547, File 127-33, Vol. 1A.

[28]Ibid.

Chapter 10

[1]*Universal Declaration of Human Rights,* General Assembly of the United Nations, December 10, 1941.

[2]S.J.C. 1946, p. iv. The Special Joint Committee of the Senate and the House of Commons appointed to examine and consider the Indian Act.

[3]Ibid., p. 1.

[4]Ibid., p. 39.

[5]For example, at Tobique Reserve, New Brunswick, in 1978, several status Indian

women have complained that they have no rights to hold property and are left destitute on marriage break-up. *The Globe and Mail,* October 24, 1977.

[6]Rowbotham, Sheila, op. cit., see Chapter 4.

[7]DIAND, Memoranda re. Amendments to the Indian Act. Ottawa-1955-56 (Blue Books v. II).

[8]S.J.C. 1946, p. 1708.

[9]Ibid., p. 762-770.

[10]P.A.C. R.G. 10 577-127-33, vol. 1A.

[11]MacInnes, T. L. R., "Canada's Indian Problem", Radio Talk, n.d.

[12]See p.

[13]S.J.C. 1946, p. 186, 152.

[14]Ibid., p. 187-190.

[15]Ibid.

[16]Ibid.

Chapter 11

[1]*House of Commons Debates,* 1950, p. 3946-73.

[2]Ibid., p. 3976.

[3]*The Indian Act,* s.c. 1951, c. 149.

[4]Ibid., s. 25, s. 49, s. 50, s. 111.

[5]Membership Division, DIAND, have very kindly provided this information and much of the information in this chapter in interviews during September, October, November 1977.

[6]*Attorney General for Canada V. Lavell, Isaac et al. V. Bedard* (1973).

[7]IRIW members in interviews. Information on this issue proved difficult to obtain. At Hobbema and Sarnia there were problems. See also Sissons, Jack, *Judge of the Far North* (Toronto: McClelland and Stewart, 1973), p. 50.

[8]Memorandum of July 2, 1969, DIAND.

[9]*The Indian Act,* s.c. 1951, c. 149, s. 109(1).

[10]Ibid., s. 109(2).

[11]*An Act to amend the Indian Act,* s.c. 1956, c. 40, s. 26.

[12]DIAND, Memoranda re. Amendments to the Indian Act, 1955-56, op. cit.

[13]This information was obtained in interviews with officials of the Membership Division, DIAND, and IRIW.

[14]DIAND, Memoranda re. Amendments to Indian Act, 1955-56, op. cit.

[15]*An Act to amend the Indian Act,* s.c. 1956, c. 40, s.3.(2).

[16]Ibid., 1956, c. 40, s.6.(5).

[17]*The Indian Act,* s.c. 1951, c. 149, s.15.

[18]Hughes, David R., and Kallen, E., *The Anatomy of Racism: Canadian Dimensions* (Montreal: Harvest House, 1974), p. 120.

[19]Interviews with DIAND officials, September — December 1977.

[20]These women have had their names deleted from the Band List following on their marriage to a non-Indian, but the next step, the Order in Council declaring them to be enfranchised, has not been taken.

²¹Starblanket, Noel, President of the NIB, in an interview, November 2, 1977.

²²Interviews with Membership Division, DIAND, October 1977.

Chapter 12

¹The Membership Division of the Lands and Membership Branch of DIAND have very kindly supplied most of the data in this chapter.

²Both men and women can enfranchise voluntarily. Involuntary enfranchisement means here Indian women's loss of status on marrying a non-Indian.

³IRIW members from Alberta, in interviews, September, October 1977.

⁴This is the writer's present understanding of the process but DIAND refused to supply any concrete information on this.

⁵For example, *The Globe and Mail* of March 6, 1978, states that on the Hobbema Reserve in Alberta royalty payments of $100 are paid several times a year and there is also a regular monthly royalty cheque of $50 per person.

⁶This information courtesy of Membership Division, DIAND.

⁷McCrossan, R. G., *The Future Petroleum Provinces of Canada — Their Geology and Potential,* Memoir 1 (Calgary: Canadian Society of Petroleum Geologists, 1973).

⁸DIAND *Indian Education in Canada* (Ottawa: Information Canada, 1973), p. 41.

⁹Ibid., p. 3.

¹⁰Ibid., p. 6-7.

¹¹Interviews with officials in Education Branch, DIAND, September-November 1977.

¹²DIAND, Annual Report, 1975-76, p. 33.

¹³DIAND Communiqué 1-7750 (Ottawa, September 1, 1977).

¹⁴Ibid.

¹⁵Tobique women made their case public at the IRIW National Conference, October 21-24, 1977.

¹⁶Louis, Edna M., *The Indian Housing Program and Indian Women* (Ottawa: DIAND, 1976), p. 3.

¹⁷The divorced or widowed spouse of a status Indian who gained Indian status through marrying an Indian retains her Indian status and all Indian rights.

¹⁸DIAND, *Cooperation Towards Partnership* (Ottawa, 1977), p. 9.

¹⁹Vandenburgh, R. M., *I am Nokomis, too, The biography of Verna Patronella Johnston* (Don Mills: General Publishing, 1977).

²⁰Campbell, Maria, *Halfbreed* (Toronto: McClelland and Stewart, 1973).

²¹IRIW members in interviews, August — December 1977.

²²*Speaking Together. Canada's Native Women,* Government of Canada, Secretary of State (Ottawa, 1975). Biography of Kahn-Tineta Miller, p. 88.

²³*Attorney-General of Canada v. Lavell.*

²⁴Ibid., esp. documentation on Yvonne Bedard.

²⁵IRIW members in interviews, August — December 1977.

²⁶Will dated December 6, 1971, was kindly provided by Cecilia Pronovost.

²⁷Xerox copies of these documents were also obtained from DIAND.

[28]It is a moot point whether the will of an Indian may be set aside by the Department in this way.

[29]Margaret Charlie was in fact certified 5 years previous to this as being "acutely psychotic", "a chronic patient" and "completely bedridden" in Katen Memorial Hospital (Doctor's certificate, November 18, 1971).

[30]Letter from Mohawk Council of Kanawake, Caughnawaga, to Cecile Pronovost, July 27, 1977, August 25, 1977.

[31]Letter from DIAND, Administrator of Estates, to D. Babits (per J. Wilkins), August 15, 1977.

[32]On June 16, 1977, V. Foy Poulin was appointed administrator of Margaret Charlie's estate by the Department.

[33]Letter from the Band Council to Cecilia Pronovost, August 24, 1977.

[34]IRIW members, and telephone interviews with officers of DIAND and Department of Justice.

[35]What force the ruling in 1949 of Deputy Minister Varcoe has in 1978 is also open to question. Another argument has been advanced in a letter to IRIW from Government in reply to a telegram that the disposition of the estate followed Quebec law.

Chapter 13

[1]Hawthorn, H. B., op. cit., vol. 1, p. 260.

[2]Ibid., p. 257.

[3]Ibid., p. 13.

[4]Ibid., p. 361.

[5]Ibid., p. 360.

[6]Government of Canada, *Statement of the Government of Canada on Indian Policy, 1969* (Ottawa, 1969), p. 3.

[7]National Indian Brotherhood, *Statement on the Proposed New "Indian Policy"*, press release, July 26, 1969.

[8]Ibid., p. 5.

[9]Government of Canada, *Statement of the Government of Canada on Indian Policy, 1969*, p. 11.

[10]Cumming, Peter A., and Mickenberg, Neil H., op. cit., p. 263.

[11]Ibid.

Chapter 14

[1]Royal Commission on the Status of Women, *Report of the Royal Commission on the Status of Women* (Ottawa: Information Canada, 1970), p. 237-8.

[2]*Canadian Bill of Rights,* s.c. 1960, c. 44, R.S.C. 1970, Appendix III.

[3]Ibid.

[4]Tarnopolsky, Walter, *The Canadian Bill of Rights* (Toronto: McClelland and Stewart, 1975) provides detailed background and analysis of all cases that relate to the Canadian Bill of Rights.

[5]Ibid., p. 128-140.

[6]Sanders, Douglas, "The Bill of Rights and Indian Status", *U.B.C. Law Review,* Vol. 7 (1972), p. 81.

[7]Cardinal, Harold, *The Unjust Society* (Edmonton: Hurtig, 1969), p. 140.

[8]Courchene, Dave, press release, June 26, 1969, p. 3.

[9]Indian Chiefs of Alberta. *Citizens Plus* (The Red Paper). June 1970.

[10]Ibid p. 4.

[11]Ibid., p. 4-5.

[12]Cheda, Sherrill, "Indian Women", in Stephenson, Marylee, ed., *Women in Canada*, revised ed. (Toronto: General Publishing Company, 1977), p. 203.

[13]Government of Canada, Secretary of State, *Speaking Together: Canada's Native Women*, p. 94.

[14]Ibid.

[15]See Tarnopolsky, Walter, op. cit., p. 149, for facts of this case.

[16]*Attorney General for Canada v. Lavell, Isaac et al. v. Bedard,* Supreme Court of Canada, 1973.

[17]Chrétien, Hon. Jean, quoted in *The Toronto Globe and Mail,* November 29, 1971, replying to a position paper from the Association of Iroquois and Allied Indians who said that 12(1)(b) was "merely a legislative embodiment of Indian custom".

[18]Interviews with Professor of Law George Neuspiel and DIAND lawyer, October 1977, February 1978.

[19]IRIW members at Caughnawaga.

[20]Cardinal, Harold, *The Rebirth of Canada's Indians* (Edmonton: Hurtig, 1977), p. 190-191.

[21]Ibid., p. 185.

[22]Ibid., p. 111.

[23]Cheda, Sherrill, op. cit., p. 204.

[24]Cardinal, Harold, *The Rebirth of Canada's Indians* (Edmonton: Hurtig, 1977), p. 112.

[25]Manuel, George, op. cit., p. 241.

[26]"Indian status case to go to top court", *The Globe and Mail,* December 2, 1971.

[27]Factum for the Respondent in the Supreme Court of Canada. Attorney General of Canada and Jeannette Vivian Corbiere Lavell, 3.4. "It is submitted that the Respondent has . . . been denied her right to equality before the law and the protection of the law without discrimination by reason of race and sex contrary to the Canadian Bill of Rights."

[28]Facta of Attorney General, NIB and Isaac et al v. Bedard.

[29]Supreme Court of Canada, *Reasons of the Court* in *Attorney General of Canada v. J. V. C. Lavell* and *Isaac V. Y. Bedard,* August 27, 1973, p. 19.

[30]Tarnopolsky, Walter, op. cit., p. 151.

[31]Ibid., p. 150-163.

[32]Supreme Court Judgement, *Reasons of Ritchie, J.,* August 27, 1973, p. 19.

[33]Tarnopolsky, Walter, op. cit., p. 150-163.

[34]Supreme Court Judgement in *Attorney General v. Lavell, Reasons of Laskin, J. (Dissenting),* August 27, 1973, p. 13.

[35]Ibid.

[36]Ibid.

[37]Smiley, D. V., "The Case against the Canadian Charter of Human Rights", *Canadian Journal of Political Science*, Vol. II (September 1969), p. 284.

[38]Sanders, D. E., "The Bill of Rights and Indian Status", *U.B.C. Law Review*, Vol. 7 (1972), p. 104.

[39]Factum of Attorney General, in *Attorney General v. Lavell*, p. 1.

[40]Supreme Court, Laskin, J. Reasons, op. cit., p. 13.

[41]Factum of the Attorney General, op. cit., p. 1.

[42]Factum of Isaac et al., p. 58-67, p. 74.

[43]Eg., Yvonne Bedard and Cecilia Pronovost, separated, and Mary Two Axe Early and Mary Tobin, widows in their seventies.

[44]Frideres, James, *Canada's Indians, Contemporary Conflicts* (Scarborough: Prentice Hall, 1974).

[45]Vandenburgh, R. M., op. cit., p. 235.

[46]This is not to deny the importance also of environment.

Chapter 15

[1]*House of Commons Debates*, May 25, 1977. (15:43). Justice Minister Basford states that all changes must be approved by the NIB-Cabinet Committee.

[2]Canadian Association in Support of Native Peoples, *And What About Canada's Native Peoples?* (Ottawa, 1976) p. 23.

[3]Starblanket, Noel, Interview with the Advisory Council on the Status of Women, November 9, 1977.

[4]Clause 63(2) of the *Canadian Human Rights Act* (1976-77) excludes the *Indian Act*. Indian women are now appealing to the United Nations to intervene on their behalf.

[5]*The Globe and Mail*, October 24, 1976.

[6]DIAND, *The James Bay and Northern Québec Agreement* (Ottawa, 1976), p. 22-23.

[7]Ibid., 23-24.

[8]Yukon Indian Land Claim, Document No. 3, March 8, 1977. A.1.

[9]The Indian Brotherhood of the Northwest Territories Statement of Rights, *Our Land, Our Culture, Our Future* (October 25, 1976), point 4, Obj. VIII.

[10]Métis Association of the Northwest Territories.

[11]Cardinal, Harold, *The Rebirth of Canada's Indians* (Edmonton: Hurtig, 1977), p. 122.

[12]See Chapter 4, 1844-45 Committee Report.

[13]"Indians' leaders warned to halt discrimination against women", *The Globe and Mail*, May 1977. "Rights Act criticized by Lalonde", *The Globe and Mail*, February 17, 1978.

[14]S. 63(2), *Canadian Human Rights Act*, 1976-77.

[15]*House of Commons Debates*, May 25, 1977, Statement by Gordon Fairweather, M.P.

[16]Information from IRIW and federal government officials.

[17]Cheda, Sherrill, op. cit., p. 204.

[18]Starblanket, Noel, Interview with Advisory Council on the Status of Women, November 9, 1977.

[19]Quebec Native Women's Association, *Wake Up Native Women,* report of a survey in Quebec on the membership section of the *Indian Act.* Summary of Conclusions.

[20]Ibid. One percent believed it should be through the female line only.

[21]IRIW members in interviews.

[22]House of Commons, *Minutes of Proceedings and Evidence of the Standing Committee on Indian Affairs,* May 25, 1976. IRIW press release, October 24, 1977.